Essential
Switzerland

Above: *the River Inn near Lavin*

PASSPORT BOOKS
NTC/Contemporary Publishing Group

Above: *St Bernard dog*

Front cover: *wooden chalets in mountain village; astronomical clock, Bern; traditional costume of Luzern*
Back cover: *dairy cow*

This edition first published in 2000 by Passport Books, a division of NTC/ Contemporary Publishing Group, Inc., 4255 West Touhy Avenue, Lincolnwood (Chicago), Illinois 60712–1975 U.S.A.

The contents of this publication are believed correct at the time of printing. Nevertheless, the publishers cannot accept responsibility for errors or omissions, nor for changes in details given. We are always grateful to readers who let us know of any errors or omissions
they come across, and future printings will be updated accordingly.

Published by Passport Books in conjunction with The Automobile Association of Great Britain.

Revised by Richard Sale

Library of Congress Catalog Card Number: on file
ISBN 0-658-01106-5

Colour separation: Chroma Graphics (Overseas) Pte Ltd, Singapore

Printed and bound in Italy by Printer Trento srl

Contents

This book employs a simple rating system to help choose which places to visit:

✓	'top ten'

◆◆◆   do not miss
◆◆   see if you can
◆   worth seeing if you have time

Richard Sale's Switzerland

Power to the People
Switzerland is a federation of 23 states, or cantons (to be precise there are 20 cantons and six half-cantons), each of which has its own constitution and legislature. The power this gives the individual citizen of Switzerland is best seen when the Federal Assembly, which sits in Bern, the capital, passes a law. If 50,000 people sign a petition against the law a national referendum must be held. As the Swiss are proud of saying, this system gives them the right to say No when Bern says Yes.

Swiss flag flying over Lake Thun

Within this landlocked country there are such distinctions that it seems barely credible they can be contained in so small a place. A journey of barely 100 miles (160km) takes you from the rolling, tree-clad hills of the Jura through Mittelland, a low-lying, pastoral landscape dotted with towns with ancient hearts but modern outlooks, to the Alps, where Europe's highest mountains can be found. Add a handful of lakes and some great rivers and you have a combination that offers some of the finest panoramas to be found anywhere. And, if you add a few more miles to your journey, it can include villages where four distinct languages are spoken.

The speakers of those languages, the Swiss themselves, have a reputation for being an aloof, even cold people, but that is a misunderstanding. They are an efficient people – the buses and trains run on time – and such an ordered way of life can be misinterpreted by visitors. The Swiss care intensely for their environment: not only the countryside but the

streets of villages and towns are clean and well kept. But behind the well-organised and structured façade is a kind, welcoming society. The Swiss are also keen on their health, often putting people's welfare first when considering changes, for instance banning cars from parts of inner cities.

The visitor benefits from all these aspects, whether on the ski slope, which will be well groomed and reached by good lifts; on a walk, which will be well sgned; in the pedestrian-only town centres; or in the clean, well-run hotels. Forget your preconceptions – Switzerland is a beautiful place and the Swiss will do their best to help you enjoy it to the full.

Switzerland's Features

Geography

• Area: 15,945sq miles (41,300sq km)
• Highest point: Dufourspitze at 15,203 feet (4,634m), shared with Italy. The Dufourspitze is the highest point of Monte Rosa, Europe's second highest mountain.
• Lake Geneva (Lac Léman) is the largest lake in Alpine Europe. Switzerland owns 60 per cent of the 224sq mile (581sq km) lake, the other 40 per cent being French.
• Switzerland is the birthplace of the Rhine, Europe's longest river.
• 60 per cent of Switzerland is covered by the Alps. The Swiss Alps have more 4,000m peaks than any other country, and boast two of Europe's most famous mountains, the Eiger and the Matterhorn.
• As the crow flies it is 250km from the Swiss border to the nearest sea port, Genoa in Italy.

Population

• Most of Switzerland's population of 6.9 million live in Mittelland.
• Despite being neutral and having no formal army, all fit Swiss men between the ages of 20 and 50 are reservists in the Swiss militia. The German-speaking Catholic cantons also supply the Swiss Guard, the Papal bodyguard.

Language

• Switzerland has four official languages: German (spoken by about 65 per cent of the population), French (20 per cent), Italian (10 per cent) and Romansch (5 per cent).

Economy

• The three most important industries are chemical/pharmaceutical, machine-tool production and clock and watchmaking.
• Some 40 per cent of the world's personal savings are in Swiss banks. Not surprisingly, banking, financial services and insurance are a major source of the country's wealth.
• On the food front, Gruyère and Emmental cheese are famous exports, not to mention chocolate: it's said that on average every man, woman and child eats at least two bars a week.

The village of Mürren, backed by the Jungfrau range

Flags

The Swiss flag is a white cross on a red background. If the colours are reversed you get the flag of the Red Cross. The Red Cross was founded by Swiss Jean Henri Dunant in the 1860s after he witnessed the suffering of the wounded after the Battle of Solferino. Dunant shared the first Nobel Peace Prize in 1901.

Confederatio Helvetica

Switzerland's post and car plate designation is CH, which stands for Confederatio Helvetica, the Helvetii being the Celtic tribe that settled the country in about 200 BC.

Essence of Switzerland

The watchmaking industry has earned Switzerland the occasional title of timekeeper of the world. But the title is also a reflection of the speed (and success) with which the country has overcome its difficulties – the mountains that cut it off, its lack of resources, and the decision not to join the European Union despite the effect that had on trade. Yet the visitor must take time to explore the country. Switzerland is not best seen in a hurry – take a walk in the mountains, perhaps lingering over a hot chocolate in a cosy chalet, or explore the medieval heart of an old town.

Below: *Zähringer Fountain backed by Bern's picturesque clock tower*
Bottom: *the romantically sited Château de Chillon at Montreux*

THE **10** ESSENTIALS

If you only have a short time to visit Switzerland, or would like to get a rounded impression of the country, here are the essentials:

From the Schilthorn there are splendid views across to the Eiger, Mönch and Jungfrau

• **Visit a mountain top.** The views are magnificent, and reaching the top can be an adventure in itself – take the rack railway to the Jungfraujoch or the cable-car over the vast drops that fall from the Schilthorn (➤ 38).

• **Visit an old town.** The medieval centres of many towns are a delight. Try Basel (➤ 12) or Bern (➤ 27), or a less well-known place like Baden (➤ 12).

• **Take a walk** to enjoy the views and the scenery. Take the Gornergrat railway from Zermatt to Riffelalp (➤ 67) and walk to Grünsee for impressive views of the Matterhorn. Or hop on the bubble lift from Grindelwald to First (➤ 37) and walk to Bachalpsee for views of the Eiger and Jungrau.

• **Go to a yodelling concert.** Yodelling was invented to communicate over great distances in the mountains but has evolved into an art form. It has an eerie, haunting sound, especially when performed out of doors at night by a male choir.

• **Visit a *Landsgemeinde.*** Switzerland is one of the last countries to preserve a local form of democracy. In a few places, such as Appenzell on the last Sunday in April, the local population gathers to hear arguments and vote on issues.

• **Enjoy a fondue.** Even the Swiss would not claim a world-class culinary reputation, but they did invent fondue and, in Gruyères and Emmental, produce the perfect cheese bases.

• **Visit an old mountain village.** Get away from modern purpose-built resorts and discover 'secret' places such as Achseten in the Bernese Oberland.

• **Eat chocolate.** All those pretty cows raised on healthy grass and air of alpine meadows provide the milk for one of the world's great chocolates.

• **Try a local carnival,** remarkable for their uninhibited joy. The most famous is at Basel (starting on the first Monday of Lent) but there are others in May.

• **Buy a souvenir.** Ever practical, the Swiss offer useful rather than ornamental souvenirs – how about a Swiss army knife, or a Swatch?

Local architecture in Foroglio in Val Bavona

The Shaping of Switzerland

200 BC
What is now Switzerland is settled by the Helvetii, a Celtic tribe from east of the Rhine. They are in turn are driven out by the Alamans.

1st century AD
Switzerland becomes the Roman province of Helvetia.

5th century
Following the fall of the Roman Empire western Switzerland is settled by the Burgundians, while the Alamans recover the east.

530
The Franks conquer Switzerland. Later the country forms part of Frankish Charlemagne's Holy Roman Empire.

11th–13th centuries
After the fall of the Frankish Empire Switzerland is divided between Germanic noble families, one of which is the Habsburgs.

1191
Bern founded.

1264
Count Rudolf III of Habsburg gradually wins control of most of Switzerland.

1291
Rudolf dies and though he leaves his Swiss holdings to his sons, the three original 'forest' cantons of Schwyz, Unterwalden and Uri agree an alliance to resist Habsburg domination. The document on which the alliance is recorded names the Confederation of Helvetica. The famous story of William Tell and his apple shoot is set during the struggle for independence.

1315
The Confederation defeats Duke Leopold's

Sixteenth-century Protestant reformer, Jean Calvin

Habsburg army at the Battle of Morgarten.

1386
The enlarged Confederation (now eight cantons) defeats the Habsburgs at the Battle of Sempach.

15th century
The Confederation is enlarged and, by signing treaties with Austria and France and fighting against the Italians, consolidates its borders.

16th century
The Reformation sweeps through Switzerland. In 1536 Jean Calvin flees from Paris to Geneva, the city then becoming the centre for Calvinism.

1618–48
Switzerland remains neutral during the Thirty Years War. Neutrality is confirmed at the Münster Conference of 1648. Though the country is necessarily involved in the Napoleonic conflicts, this sets the seal on Swiss neutrality.

1798
France occupies Switzerland and dissolves the Confederation.

1803
Napoleon reforms the Confederation, but Geneva and the Valais (Wallis) remain French. Napoleon builds a road over the Simplon Pass.

1815
The Congress of Vienna re-establishes Switzerland with 22 cantons, and also cedes the Swiss part of the French Jura to the Swiss. Swiss neutrality is reaffirmed, and later guaranteed in Paris.

1846–8
Religious divisions result in the Sonderbund War, a civil war of limited fighting. The war ends with the adoption of a new constitution that creates a federal state of 22 sovereign cantons and introduces central secular rule.

1864
The Geneva Convention codifies the 'rules' of war, and the Red Cross is formed, both on initiatives of Jean Henri Dunant.

1914–19
The Swiss remain neutral throughout World War I. After the war the League of Nations is set up in Geneva.

1939–45
Switzerland remains neutral during World War II. In subsequent years Swiss neutrality makes it a favoured place for international organisations.

1978
Jura becomes the 23rd canton.

1992
Switzerland decides not to join the EC, but does become a member of the IMF and the World Bank.

1995
The International Trade Organisation is formed,based in Geneva.

Headquarters of the International Trade Organisation

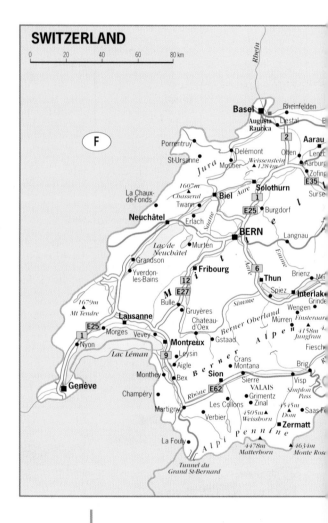

SWITZERLAND

0   20   40   60   80 km

F

Rhein

Basel ■   Rheinfelden

Augusta
Raurica   Liestal

Porrentruy   Delémont   Olten   Lenz

2   **Aarau**

St-Ursanne   Moutier   *Weissenstein*   Aarburg

Jura   ▲ *1284m*   **E35**

Zofing

1607m   *Aare*   **Solothurn**   Surse

La Chaux-
de-Fonds   ▲ *Chasseral*   **Biel**

1

Twann   **E25**   Burgdorf

Neuchâtel   Erlach   **BERN**

*Lac de
Neuchâtel*   Murten   Langnau

Grandson   *Emme*

Yverdon-
les-Bains   ■ **Fribourg**

12   *Aare*   **6**

E27   **Thun**   Brienz   Me

1679m   Bulle   Spiez   **Interlak**
▲
Mt Tendre   *Simme*   Wengen   Grinde

Lausanne   Gruyères   Chateau-
d'Oex   Mürren   *Finsteraar*

E25   *Berner Oberland*   *Alpen*   ▲ *4158m*   *4*
1   Morges   Vevey   *Jungfrau*
● Nyon   **Montreux**   Gstaad

Lac Léman   **9**   Leysin   Fiesch

Aigle   Crans   Brig

Monthey ●   Bex   *B e r n e r*   Montana   *Simplon
Pass*

Champéry ●   *Rhône*   **E62**   **Sion**   Sierre   Visp

Genève ■   **VALAIS**   ● Grimentz   ● Saas-Fe

Martigny ●   Les Collons   ● Zinal   *4515m* ▲
Weisshorn   *Dom*

Verbier   *1505m* ▲   ■ **Zermatt**

La Fouly ●   *A l p i*   *p e n n i n e*

4478m ▲   ▲ *4634m*
Matterhorn   *Monte Rosa*

*Tunnel du
Grand St-Bernard*

NORTHERN SWITZERLAND

Zürich, the country's biggest city, is the focal point of German-speaking Switzerland, which occupies much of the northern part of the country. The northeast borders the Bodensee, fringed by attractive towns and villages, while the gateway to the strategically important northwest is the fascinating city of Basel, noted for its carnival and wealth of monuments and museums.

◆◆◆ (summer)
◆ (winter)
BADEN

The health resort of Baden is worth visiting even if you are not interested in 'taking the waters', since it enjoys a delightful location in the foothills of the Jura. Known in Roman times as Aquae Helveticae, over the centuries its hot curative sulphur springs, gushing forth at 48°C (118°F), have attracted those seeking relief from rheumatism and respiratory disorders. The resort remains well equipped with excellent hotels and pleasant parks, as well as a casino. Baden's picturesque old town, the core of the medieval settlement, contains much of interest, including a covered wooden bridge (Holzbrücke) built in 1810 which leads across the **River Limmat** to the old governor's residence, now housing the **Historical Museum** and containing displays of pottery from the area, antiques, armour and excavated coins. The spa itself is attractively laid out, with pretty gardens, while resort facilities include indoor and outdoor tennis courts, fishing,

and an open air swimming pool. The Limmat-Promenade along the river is a pleasant walk.

Hotels

The **Hotel du Parc**, attractively located between the park and the thermal baths at Römer Strasse 24, and the stately **Verenahof**, are both recommended. The **Hirschen** is cheap and cheerful.

Walks and Excursions

Baden is a good base for walks and climbs in the **Lagern hills**, and also for excursions to **Habsburg Castle**, about ten minutes away, which was the ancestral seat of the Habsburgs, or, 2 miles (3km) south of Baden, to the old Cistercian **Abbey of Wettingen**, which has been converted into a school for teachers. Six miles (9km) northwest of Baden lies **Brugg**, noteworthy for its bridge and 'back tower' dating from the 11th century.

Tourist Office: Bahnhofstrasse 50 (tel: (056) 222 5318)

◆◆◆ (summer)
◆◆◆ (winter)
BASEL (Basle)

This versatile city, the northwestern gateway to Switzerland, is a place of multiple aspects and great variety. The university, founded in 1460, is Switzerland's oldest and perhaps most prestigious; the numerous museums and art galleries are known far and wide; and fascinating old buildings and a wealth of monuments lend the city dignity and charm.

Yet Basel is also a lively, progressive place, a great financial and industrial centre, renowned not only for its attractive stores and boutiques but also for its outstanding research and conference facilities.

More than 500 years ago from 1431 to 1448, the churchmen of Europe assembled at the Ecumenical Council of Basel. Today, scientists and researchers, businessmen and bankers, academics and artists meet here at conferences, seminars and specialist exhibitions. The Swiss Industries Fair alone accounts for over one million visitors a year.

Old Basel's western gateway is the splendid fortified Spalentor

Maybe the people in the frontier city are more outward-looking, more receptive to innovation than most. Sharing some of the characteristics of three nations – Switzerland, Germany and France – they cherish their own way of life. Even the famous *Fasnacht*, or carnival, has its own peculiar quality, as do many other Basel customs. Basel is a modern city, yet has contrived to preserve most of its old town, widely considered one of the finest in Europe. The view of the cathedral from the right bank (**Kleinbasel**) is particularly impressive, as is that from the **Pfalz** (cathedral promontory) back over Kleinbasel. Then there are the picturesque Gothic sections of town with magnificent fountains, the market square in front of the imposing **Rathaus** (town hall) and the **Spalentor**, the city's western gateway and reputedly the most beautiful in Switzerland.

Places of Interest

Basel's rich, extensive range of museums houses some of the world's most prestigious collections of old and new masterpieces. Within easy walking distance are more than 30 lively and interesting museums.

Kunstmuseum (Museum of Fine Arts), St Alban-Graben 16. This is the pride and joy of Basel's museums and said to be the oldest public art collection in the world, dating from 1662. It is rich in old masters such as Witz, the Holbeins, Grünewald and Manuel as well as great collections of 19th- and 20th-century art.
Open: daily except Mondays.

Museum für Gegenwartskunst (Museum of Contemporary Art), St Alban Rheinweg 60. Widely recognised as Europe's leading museum of art of the 1960s, 1970s and 1980s, it features such artists as Frank Stella, Donald Judd, Bruce Nauman, Richard Long and Jonathan Borofsky.
Open: daily except Mondays.

Historisches Museum, Barfüsserkirche, Barfüsserplatz. A 14th-century Franciscan church has been transformed into a historical museum housing the cathedral treasures, riches of the Basel guilds. Gothic sculptures and tapestries.
Open: daily except Tuesdays.

Monuments: Basel's other fine monuments include the **Münster** (Cathedral), founded in 1019 by the Emperor Henry II; the **Predigerkirche** or **Dominican Church** (1269); the **Rathaus** (town hall) of 1504–14; and town mansions and corporate houses from the 15th and 16th centuries.

Tierpark (Zoo). Here, some 5,500 animals and 600 different species live in a magnificent park in the middle of the city. A special part of the zoo is put aside for children.

Guided sightseeing tours by coach, depart daily from the Hotel Victoria (near the railway station SBB) at 10.00hrs. Also, accompanied walks through the old city and excursions to the countryside around Basel are organised by the Basel Tourist Board all year round.

Basel Carnival

There can be remarkably few annual revelries that start at the ungodly hour of 04.00hrs, especially on a chilly Monday in February or early March. The Basler *Fasnacht* is one of them. Not content with that, it lasts for three days and three whole nights, which is enough for anyone to warm up and let off steam… The *Fasnacht*, described by locals as the best free show of the year', begins on the Monday following Ash Wednesday.

The musicians' fantastic masks and costumes set the tone for Basel's three-day madness at Fasnacht

Numerous carnival associations parade through the narrow streets of the old town. Wearing grotesque masks and with small lanterns perched on their heads, come pipers and drummers, holding huge transparent lanterns with the emblem of their particular association in caricature. This curious parade lasts until dawn. On Monday and Wednesday afternoons the associations, or *cliques* as they are known, with their fifes and drums, again march through the streets.

On the Tuesday the carnival lanterns are exhibited at the Basler Halle, which normally houses part of the Swiss Industries Fair. The exhibition is well worth a visit, for many of the lanterns are real works of art, designed by the best local artists.

Events of the Wednesday, the third and last day of the *Fasnacht*, are similar to those of Monday but without the opening ceremony. The fun reaches its climax in the evening and lasts until the early hours of Thursday morning, when Basel goes back to work again… and starts looking forward to next year's carnival!

Hotels

The de luxe class **Drei Könige am Rhein** at Blumenrain 8, which flanks the Rhein and is only five minutes from the market place, is excellent; also the moderately

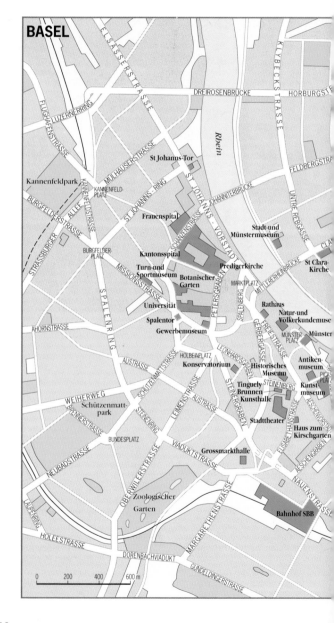

BASEL

ELSÄSSERSTRASSE
FLUGHAFENSTRASSE
LUZERNERRING
MÜLHAUSERSTRASSE
DREIROSENBRÜCKE
HORBURGST
KLYBECKSTRASSE
Rhein
St Johanns-Tor
Kannenfeldpark
KANNENFELD-PLATZ
KANNENFELDSTRASSE
BURGFELDERSTRASSE
STRASSBURGER ALLEE
ST JOHANNS-RING
ST JOHANNS-VORSTADT
JOHANNITERBRÜCKE
SCHANZENSTRASSE
FELDBERGSTRA
UNTRE REBGASSE
Frauenspital
Stadt-und
Münstermuseum
CLA
BURGFELDER-PLATZ
Kantonsspital
Predigerkirche
St Clara-Kirche
MISSIONSSTRASSE
Turn-und
Sportmuseum
Botanischer
Garten
PETERSGRABEN
MARKTPLATZ
MITTLERE RHEINBRÜCKE
SPALENRING
Universität
SPALENBERG
SPALENVORSTADT
Rathaus
Natur-und
Völkerkundemuse
AHORNSTRASSE
Spalentor
Gewerbemuseum
FREIE STRASSE
GERBERGASSE
MÜNSTER
PLATZ
Münster
LEONHARDSGRABEN
HÖLBEINPLATZ
Antiken-
museum
AUSTRASSE
SCHÜTZENMATTSTRASSE
Konservatorium
Historisches
Museum
PICA
LATZ
LEIMENSTRASSE
Tinguely
Brunnen
STEINENBERG
Kunst-
museum
WEIHERWEG
Schützenmatt-
park
BRENNERSTRASSE
STEINENRING
AUSTRASSE
Kunsthalle
Stadttheater
ELISABE THANSTRASSE
AESCHENGRABEN
Haus zum
Kirschgarten
BUNDESPLATZ
NEUBADSTRASSE
OBERWILERSTRASSE
VIADUKTSTRASSE
Grossmarkthalle
AESCHENGRABEN
NAUENSTRASSE
LAUFENRING
Zoologischer
Garten
MARGARETHENSTRASSE
Bahnhof SBB
HOLEESTRASSE
DORENBACHVIADUKT
GUNDELDINGERSTRASSE

0   200   400   600 m

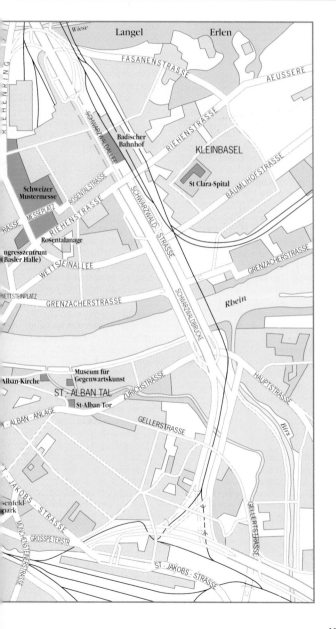

priced riverside **Hecht am Rhein Hotel** at Rheingasse 8. Worth a try also, for its real decorative character is the **Temfelhof.**

Entertainment

One of the most popular places for an evening drink is the **Café des Arts at Stadt-Casino** in the Barfüsserplatz. Try too the stylish bar in the **Hotel Euler**, and, if you're into live loud music, the **Café Atlantis** in Klosterberg.

Restaurants

One of the best in the city is **La Rotisserie des Rois** in the **Drei Konige Hotel**, which has a wonderful atmosphere and serves excellent food. Also recommended is the **St Alban-Stübli**, which offers good food at reasonable prices in a delightful part of the old town.

Shopping

The fashionable shopping street of Basel is the Freie Strasse, leading to the marketplace and town hall. And the fleamarket, on Saturdays at Petersplatz, is a popular hunting ground for the curio-lovers.

Excursions

A popular excursion from Basel is to **Augusta Raurica**, the site of a Roman colony founded in 27BC. Of particular interest are the theatre and the remains of several temples, as well as the museum located within a reconstruction of a Roman house. Basel is also a good base for exploring other regions and villages of northwest Switzerland, many of them with old castles, such as

Lenzburg. Likewise the towns of **Aarau**, **Aarburg** and **Zofingen** all have a rich historic past and are well worth visiting. Around **Liestal** the countryside is delightful in spring, when thousands of cherry trees break into blossom.

Tourist Office: Blumenrain 2, CH-4001 Basel (tel: (061) 261 5050)

◆◆◆ (summer)
◆ (winter)
SCHAFFHAUSEN ✓

Capital of Switzerland's northernmost canton, Schaffhausen, wonderfully set on terrraces on the right bank of the Rhein, contains some of the country's most impressive ancient buildings. The majority of these 16th- to 18th-century buildings – richly embellished with statues, reliefs, frescos and oriel windows – are found in the old town centre, which is a pedestrian-only zone. Particularly impressive are the late Renaissance frescos on the **Haus zum Ritter** (Knight's House) and the richly decorated façade of the **Haus zum Goldenen Ochsen** (Golden Ox). In the public squares are historic fountains, and no fewer than 12 guildhalls, some now restaurants, attest to the prosperity of their masters. The ancient heart of the town was the street market, located in what is now the Vordergasse. Presiding over all is St John's church, noted for its excellent acoustics. Music-lovers continue to delight in its Good Friday concerts as well as the Bach Festival held every three years.

A fine view of the Rhein is had from Schaffhausen's Munot Fortress

Places of Interest

Museum zu Allerheiligen (All Saints' Museum). Its rooms contain a notable cultural and historical collection, including prehistoric collections from local excavations. Virtually all the manuscripts of the former Benedictine library are preserved in the city library located in the old granary (Kornhaus) of the cloister complex. *Open*: daily except Mondays.

Münster (All Saints' Church). This 11th-century church built of yellow ochre coloured stone is one of the best examples of Romanesque architecture in Switzerland, and today houses a school of music. In the adjoining medieval herb garden the various plants and seedlings are identified in careful script.

Munot Fortress. Superb views of the town and its surroundings can be enjoyed from the Munot Fortress which overlooks Schaffhausen. The top of the fortress is reached by climbing a spiral ramp inside the keep. It was built between 1564 and 1585 and the watchman and his family still live in the tower. Every evening at 21.00hrs he rings the bell – once the signal to close the town gates and public houses.

Rheinfall. Nearby Neuhausen contains what are said to be the most powerful waterfalls in Europe – the Rheinfall (Falls of the Rhein), with a height of 75 feet (23m). On a platform extending over a part of the basin, spectators can experience the water thundering beneath their feet and swirling around them. For the truly courageous there is even a small boat which goes to the rock formation at the foot of the falls. The spectacle is best seen during high water in summer, in July particularly.

Hotels and Restaurants

The **Hotel Parkvilla** at Parkstrasse 18 is elegantly furnished, while the **Bellevue** has an attractive terrace. The **Rheinhotel Fischerzunft** has an excellent reputation for cuisine.

Tourist Office: Fronwagturm 12, CH-8201 Schaffhausen (tel: (056) 225 5141)

The seething rush of the mighty Rheinfall near Schaffhausen

◆◆◆ (summer)
◆◆ (winter)
SOLOTHURN ✓

Solothurn's reputation as Switzerland's best-preserved and most beautiful baroque town is well earned. One of the oldest towns north of the Alps, its name is of Celtic origin. The Romans built a fort here, traces of which can still be seen.

In this small area, the visitor can study sacred buildings of European importance such as the 17th-century **Jesuitenkirche** (Jesuits' Church) or the 18th-century **St Ursenkathedrale** (Cathedral of St Ursus), as well as the seats of patrician families, charming burghers' houses, forbidding military defences, of which the **Krummturm** (Crooked Tower) is the most striking feature, and beautiful old fountains.

Museums

The **Kunstmuseum** (Museum of Fine Art) has an impressive collection of post-1850 Swiss art and old masters.
Open: daily except Mondays.
The **Naturmuseum** (Natural History Museum) is a joy for children to visit, as they may both see and touch the exhibits.
Open: daily except Mondays.
One of Europe's largest collections of weapons is to be seen in the **Altes Zeughaus** (old Arsenal Museum).
Open: daily except Mondays; weekday mornings in winter.
The **Historisches Museum Blumenstein** (just outside the town centre) shows how the ruling classses lived.
Open: daily except Mondays.

Sport

For sports enthusiasts there are facilities for tennis, squash, riding, swimming and miniature golf in the town and its immediate surroundings. In summer, the **Weissenstein/ Balmberg** area is ideal for walks and hikes, and in winter there is skiing and cross-country skiing as well as tobogganing.

Hotels

The **Krone (Couronne)** at Hauptgasse 64, one of the oldest inns in Switzerland, is the best hotel in town. A little less expensive, the **Roter Turm/Tour Rouge**, has a bowling alley.

Restaurants

The **Zunfthaus zu Wirthen**, situated in the old town guildhouse at Hauptgasse 41, serves seasonal dishes made from fresh local produce.
Baseltor, Hauptgasse 79, is a restaurant/grill that enjoys a fine reputation in historic surroundings. **Hardy's**, Stalen 35, has a pleasant terrace.

Excursions

Numerous excursions are possible in the immediate vicinity, such as to the **hermitage in the Verena gorge**; to the oldest and most important **stork settlement** in Switzerland, in Altreu; and to Solothurn's 'local' mountain, the **Weissenstein** whose peak – reached by chairlift – offers an incomparable view across the swiss Mittelland to the snow-covered Alpine chain.
The Lake of Biel (Bieler See), the Bernese Oberland, Central Switzerland, Bern, Basel, Luzern, Zürich and Neuchâtel are all within easy reach.

Tourist Office: Hauptgasse 69, CH-4500 Solothurn (tel: (032) 626 4646)

♦♦♦ (summer)
♦♦♦ (winter)

ZÜRICH

Although Switzerland's largest city is small by world standards, with a population of around 400,000, it nevertheless boasts all the advantages of an international metropolis, together with an attractive location at the northern end of Lake Zürich (Zürichsee). Switzerland's most important centre of commerce, banking and industry – silk, cotton, machinery, paper and food – Zürich is also a main cultural centre of German-speaking Switzerland.

Sightseeing

Walking is the best way to get to know the attractive old town. The **Lindenhof** is a good starting point and offers an attractive view over the old town. In 15BC the Romans built a customs post here, thereby founding Turicum, now known as Zürich. However, Zürich was not recorded as a town in official documents until the year 929. In 1336 aritsans organised in guilds took over the government of the city; nowadays these guilds appear in public just once a year, on the third Monday in April, when the spring festival known as *Sechseläuten* is held. Clad in traditional guild costumes, the men parade around the city, arriving at **Sechseläutenplatz** towards evening. In a show almost medieval in character, a cotton-wool snowman symbolising winter is burnt on a giant bonfire, while bands of guild horsemen gallop around his place of execution.

The modern city silhouette is dominated by the striking towers and spires of three old churches – the **Grossmünster**, endowed by Charlemagne; **St Peterskirche**, which boasts Europe's largest clock face (28½ feet/8.6 metres), and the **Fraumünster**, greatly admired for its stained-glass windows by Marc Chagall (completed 1970). An important milestone in Zürich's development into an important international financial, economic and trade centre was the foundation of the Zürich Stock Exchange (**Börse**) in 1877, now the world's fourth most important.

Hotels

The **Baur au Lac Hotel**, Talstrasse 1, with its lovely garden, superb restaurant and high standards, is one of the best hotels in Switzerland. Also first-rate are the **Savoy Hotel Baur en Ville**, Am Paradeplatz, the **Dolder Grand Hotel**, Kurhausstrasse 20, – a grand hotel in all senses of the word – and the **Eden au Lac**, Utoquai 45. Of the moderately priced establishments the family run **Hotel Leonhard**, Limmatquai, enjoys an excellent reputation, as does the budget-priced **Hotel Bristol**, Stampfenbachstrasse 34.

Culture and Entertainment

There are more than 30 museums in **Zürich** with a great variety of exhibitions. The many interesting works of art in the **Schweizerisches Landesmuseum** (Swiss National Museum) opposite the railway station, for example, provide a lively demonstration of Swiss history.

Open: daily except Mondays. The municipal theatre (**Schauspielhaus**), the Opera House (**Opernhaus**), the Concert Hall (**Tonhalle**) and various smaller theatres as well as other institutions offer a varied selection of cultural events. Culture is highlighted in the annual June Festival, whose chief characteristics are concerts, opera, ballet, drama, exhibitions and lectures, all centring on a particular theme. Full details of events in the city appear in the *Zürich Little Big City What's On*.

The twin towers of the Grossmünster watch over Zürich's river, the Limmat

Located a taxi-ride from Zürich's city centre, in Zollikerstrasse, the **Emil Bührle Collection** is an impressive collection of French paintings, particularly of the 19th century, including works by Corot, Courbet and Delacroix and Impressionist paintings by Cézanne, Degas, Gauguin, Manet, Renoir and Van Gogh. Unfortunately, there are very limited opening hours so, before making the visit, check the times in advance with the tourist office.

For those in search of nightlife, night-clubs are numerous and range from the fashionable to the folkish.

Restaurants

At the upper end of the price range the **Agnes Amberg**, Hottingerstrasse 5, and the famous **Kronenhalle** are both outstanding. Of the less expensive restaurants, the huge old **Zeughauskeller**, Am Paradeplatz, has its devotees, as does the locals' favourite, **Bierhalle Kropf**, nearby. For pastries and atmosphere, the **Schober**, in Napfgasse, is a 'must'.

Shopping

Zürich's international reputation also rests on its excellent shopping facilities and its fame

23

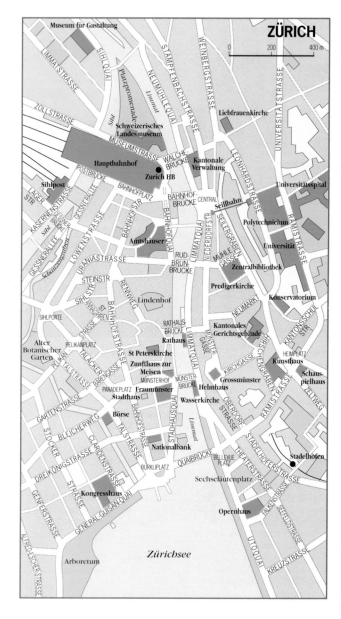

as an art dealing centre – a number of notable auction houses are based here.

With its elegant boutiques and famous *couturières* the **Bahnhofstrasse** is considered one of the most attractive shopping streets in the world, the unusual distinction of having a catacomb of bank vaults beneath it.

Excursions

Only 15 minutes from Zürich, via the expressway leading beyond the airport, lies the industrial city of **Winterthur**, noted for its impressive art collections, particularly those displayed in the **Oskar Reinhart Foundation** in Stadthausstrasse and in the villa in which the benefactor used to live in Am Romerholz. Among the paintings on display are priceless works by Brueghel, Cézanne and Van Gogh.

Open: daily except Mondays.

Other popular excursions are to **Üetliburg**, the most northern peak in the Albis ridge; the medieval village of **Regensberg**, with its half-timbered houses and imposing castle; and **Rapperswil**, known as 'the town of roses'.

Tourist Office: Hauptbahnhof, CH-8023 Zürich (tel: (01) 215 4000)

A tram in Zürich's Bahnhofstrasse; this elegant street is car-free, enhancing the pleasure of shopping

CENTRAL SWITZERLAND

This part of the country has been luring discerning travellers since long before the current fascination with skiing and winter sports. Byron, Shelley, Longfellow, Mendelssohn, Wagner and Brahms are just a few of the many famous names who have been inspired by this delightful region, which offers much in the way of interest, not least the splendid town of Luzern and the richly varied canton of Bern. To the south lies the Bernese Oberland, with its spectacular mountains, glaciers,

The Swiss capital, Bern: the country's tallest spire dominates the old town

waterfalls and lakes, plus pretty villages and holiday resorts.

◆◆ (summer)
◆◆◆ (winter)
BEATENBERG
Lying in the heart of the Swiss Alps at an altitude of 3,773 feet (1,150m), Beatenberg is one of the leading holiday resorts in the Bernese Oberland, universally popular thanks to numerous natural attractions that include its fine location, mild

climate, unrivalled view of the entire Alpine chain, and a particularly sunny situation. Beatenberg offers some 3,500 beds in hotels, inns, chalets, rented apartments and health homes that nestle among fir trees. Beneath the village lie the famous St Beatus's Caves (Beatus Höhlen).

Summer attractions include hiking paths, mini-golf, tennis and other sporting activities, and a wide-ranging programme of entertainment and excursions.

Excursion

For an unrivalled view of Beatenberg and the Alpine chain go to the top of **Niederhorn**, which is reached by chairlift. At an altitude of 6,397 feet (1,950m) there are spectacular views from viewing platforms at the top, south over Beatenberg and beyond Lake Thun to the glaciers of the Jungfrau Massif. To the southwest, Mont Blanc is just visible in the distance.

Tourist Office: Postfach 162, CH-3803 Beatenberg (tel: (033) 841 1818)

◆◆◆ (summer)
◆◆◆ (winter)
BERN (BERNE) ✓

By European standards, Bern – the capital of Switzerland – is not a big city. It has only 140,000 inhabitants, or 300,000 if you count those in the suburbs, but it is very Swiss, very Alemanic, and very picturesque.

The city was founded a century before the Swiss Confederation itself, by the last Duke of Zähringen, Berchtold V, for

strategic reasons. The duke entrusted one of his noblemen, Cuno von Budenberg, with the task of building a city here. The city was started in 1191 on the site of Nydegg Castle. Cuno built a city wall, in the centre of which rose a great Clock Tower, and in it was the main gate. In front of the city wall is a natural hollow which served as a moat. In the 13th century, under the protectorate of Count Peter of Savoy, the city's frontier was extended westwards and a new city wall, with the prison tower as its main gateway, was erected. In the 14th century there were further additions to the city, taking it to where the main station now stands.

In 1405 the greater part of the town was destroyed by fire. The houses were rebuilt on the old foundations, but instead of wood, sandstone from nearby quarries was used as building material. Most of these houses were replaced in the 16th and 17th centuries by new buildings whose harmonious appearance and richness of detail are a delight.

Bern's greatest territorial power was reached between the years 1536 and 1798, mostly gained at the cost of the House of Savoy. Large territories along Lac Léman (the Lake of Geneva) came under Bernese rule and it is chiefly thanks to Bern that much of the French part of Switzerland is today within the Confederation.

The invasion of the French in 1798 destroyed Bern's position of authority. However, it became the cantonal capital and in 1848 had the honour of being chosen by the first Swiss parliament as the capital of the Swiss Federation.

In the past fifty years Bern has expanded enormously, and wide bridges now span the Aare to link the old city with its new suburbs. While retaining its medieval appearance, the old city (Nydegg) has developed into an important business centre.

Happily sited where German-speaking Switzerland meets French, Bern has a distinct touch of the latter. A breath of Gallic spirit permeates its streets and its unostentatious baroque buildings while, in the arcades, rapid-fire French mingles with the ponderous tones of the Bern-German dialect.

City Features

Arcades. Characteristic of Bern's streets are the medieval arcades set into the façades of the buildings. Even in the worst of weathers you can walk from one end of the city to the other without getting your feet wet. The people of Bern call it *lauben* ('arcading') when they stroll through these airy vaults which open into the roadway in

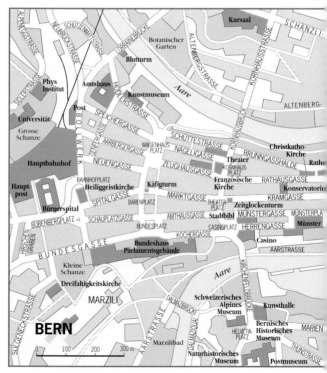

sweeping arches, while the other side is flooded with light from the stores and window displays in Europe's first and largest sheltered shopping area. The city guards its arcades with a jealous eye; no house may be rebuilt or renovated without an arcade on the ground floor, and every façade has to fit in with neighbouring ones.

Cathedral and Town Hall. High above the rooftops towers the Münster (Cathedral of St Vincent), one of the finest ecclesiastical buildings in Switzerland. Like most of Bern it dates from the 15th century.

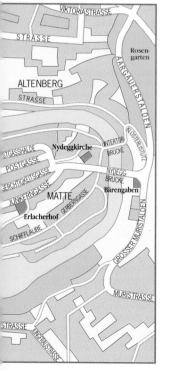

Only a few years after the fire of 1405, work began on a new town hall. Broad and solid, this Gothic building, restored to all its old splendour, stands between Rathausgasse and Postgasse. Then, five years after its completion, the citizens of Bern set about building a new cathedral. A memorial tablet gives the year the foundation stone was laid as 1421. The cathedral dominates the curve of the Aare, where the steep ramparts of the old walls plunge down to the river.

Clock Tower. The Zeitglockenturm is one of Bern's most popular attractions. Originally dating from the 12th century, it was gutted in 1405, and then rebuilt in stone. In 1530 the astronomical or calendar clock, showing the position of the sun, moon, stars and planets as well as the month and day of the week, was constructed; and at the same time the delightful mechanical figure-play was made. This includes a jester, a parade of marching bears, a cock, a knight in golden armour and Father Time.

Fountains. Below the Cathedral is Junkerngasse where the houses of the old city aristocracy stand in four-square comfort. Rathausgasse and Postgasse, which broaden out virtually into extended squares, and Kramgasse and Gerechtigkeitsgasse, with their magnificent 16th-century fountains, each with a theme, run parallel to it.

Market. Spread along streets and squares, this extends as far as the Bundesplatz, where the merry bustle surges up against the somewhat formal Swiss parliament building.

The **Kunstmuseum** (Fine Art Museum) is one of the best art galleries in Switzerland and has a particularly fine collection of works by Paul Klee.

Open: daily except Mondays

New Town

The new town, across the Aare, is accessible by four bridges. Of special interest here is the **Bundeshaus** (Federal Palace), a domed 19th-century Florentine Renaisssance-style building.

Also in the new town, the **Schweizerisches Alpines Museum** (Swiss Alpine Museum), at Helvetiaplatz 4 with the Postal Museum (below) highlights the natural history and culture of the Swiss Alps, including the history of mountaineering.

Open: daily.

The **Schweizerisches Postmuseum** (Swiss Postal Museum) focuses on the history of postal and communication services in Switzerland, plus stamps from around the world.

Open: daily except Tuesdays.

The extraordinary mock 16th-century building of the **Bernisches Historisches Museum** (Bernese Historical Museum) at Helvetiaplatz 5 is really less than a century old.

Open: daily except Mondays; free Sundays.

Close by, at Bernastrasse 15, is the **Naturhistorisches Museum** (Natural History Museum).

Open: daily. Free Wednesday, Saturday and Sunday afternoons.

Hotels

The **Schweizerhof**, Bahnhofplatz 11, is one of Switzerland's finest

hotels, with a well-deserved reputation for the standards of accommodation, service and food. Another luxury hotel is the **Bellevue Palace**, Kochergasse 3–5, while less expensive but hugely characterful is the **Goldener Schlüssel**, Rathausgasse 72.

Entertainment

Bern has a regular opera and theatre season running from late September to April. Opera and ballet are presented at the **Stadttheater** and concerts at a number of other halls. Plays are usually in German. Full details of productions are available from local tourist offices.

Restaurants

The **Schultheissenstube** at the **Schweizerhof Hotel** is expensive but generally well worth it, and also highly recommended is the very formal **Bellevue Grill** in the **Bellevue Palace Hotel**. In the moderately priced category **Harmonie**, Hotelgasse 3, is an old-world place famous for its fondues.

Excursions

Popular excursions are to the district of **Emmental**, about ten minutes away, and noted for its cheese; and to the ancient celtic city of **Thun**, which lies southeast of Bern, on Lake Thun (Thuner See), and is a summer playground for the yachting set. Other areas worth visiting are **Schwarzenburg** and **Seeland**, and the villages lying on the shores of Seeland Lake (Bieler See) such as **Twann**, **Ligerz** and **Erlach**.

Tourist Office: Im Hauptbahnhof, Bahnhofplatz, CH-3001 Bern (tel: (031) 328 1212)

Brienz is a popular summer resort

◆◆◆ (summer)
◆◆ (winter)

BRIENZ

Nestling between the upper end of lake Brienz (Brienzer See) and the southern slopes of the Brienzer Rothorn, Brienz is located nine miles (15km) east of Interlaken in the very heart of Switzerland. At 1,863 feet (568m) above sea-level it enjoys a mild mountain climate thanks to the compensating effects of the lake. It is well known for its local craft of wood-carving.

From the Brunngasse up to the old church, the village centre has been well preserved, its wooden houses in the narrow alleys ablaze with pelargoniums in the summer, while the lakeshore promenade is among the village's many delights. The lake itself is available for swimming, waterskiing, sailing, surfing or fishing, while a trip on one of its famous paddle-steamers is a delightful diversion.

An extensive network of marked

paths around the village and up into the mountains makes it easy for visitors to explore the resort's surroundings, including the neighbouring villages of Schwanden, Hofstetten and Brienzwiler.

Brienzer Rothorn Bahn

The famous steam-driven rack railway takes visitors to the top of the Brienzer Rothorn. Construction was started in 1890 and in 1891 the first engine took one hour to cover the distance of 4.7 miles (7.6km) with an average incline of 22° to the 7,710ft (2,350m) peak. Seven steam engines are in service every summer from June to October; five of them date back to 1891/92, the others to 1933 and 1936. The trip – offering panoramic views – is unforgettable. To reach the summit from the terminus there is a 15- to 20-minute walk. The Rothorn itself is the starting point for many good walks, but visitors wishing to enjoy a spectacular sunset or sunrise are advised to book a bed in the **Rothorn Kulm** mountain hotel well in advance.

Hotels

Brienz offers a range of comfortable, traditional hotels with some 500 beds, as well as apartments, a youth hostel, and camping sites. The **Seehotel Bären**, which borders the lake and has its own private beach, has a pleasant garden and terrace, as well as a swimming pool. The smaller **Hotel Schönegg** is also recommended.

Excursions

The **Axalp** lies about six miles (10km) from Brienz and can be reached by public transport, car or special excursions in the season. At some 5,250 feet (1,600m) above sea-level, it is popular in summer for relaxing, touring and walking, while overnight accommodation is available in two hotels and a tourist hostel.

Ballenberg Open Air Museum of rural dwellings and lifestyle, just northeast of Brienz, can be reached by public transport, but travel companies put on special excursion buses in the season. Here examples of houses and settlements from all parts of Switzerland have been reconstructed in an impressive park comprising seven theme areas.

The museum was opened in 1978 with 15 completed houses. Now, more than 50 buildings from various parts of Switzerland are open to the public, and plans are afoot to reconstruct a total of 100 buildings. People employed in traditional crafts such as bread-baking, cheese-making, basket-weaving, spinning, weaving and wood-carving bring the old houses to life. *Open*: daily from mid-April to October.

Tourist Office: Hauptstrasse 143, CH-3855 Brienz (tel: (033) 952 8080)

◆◆◆ (summer)
◆ (winter)

BRUNNEN

Located on the shores of Lake Luzern (Vierwaldstätter See) and framed by mountains, Brunnen is a resort with characteristic Swiss houses and shops and a lakeside promenade complete with attractive cafés.

Visitors should look out for the gaily painted water pumps dotted around the village, and be sure to visit the pretty little chapel in the centre of town. Brunnen lies at the head of Lake Uri (Urnersee), the most dramatic branch of Lake Luzern, its sheer cliffs giving it the appearance of a Norwegian fjord.

Lake Luzern itself offers a variety of activities. Steamers leaving from Brunnen call at historic sites on the lake such as William Tell's chapel and the Rütli meadow, birthplace of the Swiss Confederation.

Nearby **Flüelen** is a watersports paradise, while Brunnen itself has a lido where you can bathe in the lake or swim in the indoor pool. Sports facilities in the resort include mountain bikes, bicycles, bowling, tennis and table tennis. A fitness trail in the woods is a fun activity to try, or you can take the train to **Seedorf** for an afternoon's horse-riding. Children might enjoy the play area on the lakeside, where there are small animals to stroke and photograph.

Hotels

Recommended hotels include the **Bellevue au Lac**, an elegant establishment situated on the lakeside promenade, with magnificent views of the lakes and mountains; and the **Hotel Brunnerhof**, in the main square just a short step from the lake.

Entertainment

For evening entertainment, cruises with music and dancing are very popular, or you can try your luck in the casino. Live bands perform throughout the summer, and every week a Swiss folklore evening is held with Alpine music. The bars in

Visitors enjoy strolling along the lakeshore promenade at Brunnen

Brunnen have a continental atmosphere, and for variety you can sample a cheese fondue or pizza.

Tourist Office: Bahnhofstrasse 32, CH-6440 Brunnen (tel: (041) 825 0040)

◆◆◆ (summer)
◆◆◆ (winter)
ENGELBERG
Dominated by a 12th-century Benedictine monastery, this pretty village is set at the foot of the Titlis mountains at the heart of a beautiful valley that leads up from Lake Luzern (Vierwaldstätter See). It is a charming spot with a relaxed atmosphere.

The Titlis Glacier means that it can boast snow year-round – you can usually even enjoy limited skiing here in July! There are over 35 miles (56km) of downhill runs in three areas, with something for all grades of skier. The run from Titlis to the village is about eight miles (13km) long.

A free ski-bus service takes about three minutes to transport you from the village to the new gondola cable car that takes you up to **Gerschnialp** at 4,100 feet (1,250m), from where two further cable cars run parallel up to **Trubsee** at 6,000 feet (1,800m).

From Trubsee a two-stage cable car rises to nearly 10,000 feet (3000 metres). The second stage has the novelty of the world's first rotating cabin, allowing thrilling views of the dramatic glacial scenery.

Many of Engelberg's walking paths are close to the ski areas, so that non-skiers can meet up with family or friends at lunchtime.

The village has a good range of additional facilities, such as indoor skating and curling rinks, two tennis courts, swimming pools, tea rooms and plenty of excursions, as well as guided tours of the monastery, making it a popular resort during the summer too.

Restaurants and Entertainment
In the winter season there are après-ski get-togethers at several hotels, while every Tuesday there is a horse sleigh ride through the village followed by a fondue party. For some typical folklore try the **Bänklialp Hotel** or the restaurant **Sporthalle** where there is also a bowling alley. Engelberg has some delightful little restaurants and plenty of *Stüblis* and bars – the bar of the **Hotel Hess** is a popular meeting place and there is music and dancing at the **Carmena**, **Spindle**, **Angel Pub** and **Bierlialp**. The casino has a gaming room and night spot with dancing. The **Hotel Regina Titlis**, in the centre of town in Dorfstrasse, has a swimming pool and sauna.

Tourist Office: Klosterstrasse 3, CH-6390 Engelberg (tel: (041) 637 3737)

◆◆◆ (summer)
◆◆◆ (winter)
GRINDELWALD
Popularly known as the 'village of the glaciers', Grindelwald is situated at the foot of the north face of the Eiger on a broad, sunny plateau some 3,500 feet

The Wetterhorn broods over Grindelwald, with its typical Alpine church

(1,050m) above sea-level. The most famous and largest ski resort in the Bernese Oberland, the town is a gateway to the whole Jungfrau region with its enormous choice for intermediate and advanced skiers.

There are three main areas for good skiing. **First** is reached by chairlift from the centre of the village, **Kleine Scheidegg** by mountain railway from the station, and **Männlichen** by gondolaway which starts about five minutes by road from the centre.

In winter Grindelwald is an excellent choice for both skiers and non-skiers, but as it is the only resort in the region accessible by car, it can be very busy in peak season. Visitors should also consider carefully which ski pass to buy as there are big differences in price and validity.

Mountaineering

Grindelwald is excellent for mountaineers. The Grindelwald mountain guides have their own climbing centre, which not only offers training in rock climbing

Skiing at over 6,700 feet (2,000m) near the Kleine Scheidegg in the Bernese Oberland

and on ice, but also one- or two-day tours to the various Bernese Oberland peaks, glacier hiking and climbing weeks and, in addition, walking and hiking for senior citizens and trekking in the Alpine foothills.

Sports Facilities

For tennis fans there are 11 open air courts; and the sports centre's ice rink, open for skating from July to April, is also used for tennis in May and June. The sports centre, centrally located, also offers a sauna and solarium, fitness facilities, table tennis, a children's play area, a casino and an indoor pool. Those who prefer swimming in the sun can walk up to the Hellbach open-air pool in **Grund**. There is also a marked fitness trail for training purposes and two Alpine orienteering routes.

Courses

Those who want to look down on the world can attend

weekend courses in hang-gliding or para-gliding, while those more attracted by Alpine flora can learn more about it along the **Grütli-Waldlehrpfad**. The Heimatmuseum offers information on Grindelwald customs, the beginning of mountaineering and winter sports and on Alpine dairies and cheese-making.

Hotels

There is a wide choice of accommodation in the resort, including modern hotels with indoor pools and bars, second- and third-category hotels, family-run guest houses, charming wooden chalets and holiday apartments – more than 8,000 beds in total. The five-star **Grand Hotel Regina** has an enviable position in the village and its gardens, heated outdoor pool and sun terrace enjoy one of the most glorious Alpine backdrops imaginable. The **Hotel Belvedere** is a first-class establishment offering high standards of service and cuisine in a lovely setting. The **Fiescherblick** is a modern mountain inn offering both good value and excellent local knowledge.

Entertainment

The **Spider Club** is a lively music venue for arachnophiles, while **Herby's Bar** offers a more sophisticated atmosphere.

Restaurants

The best restaurant in town is almost certainly the **Jagerstube** at the **Regina** – it is stylish and serves delicious food. The **Alte Post** combines superb Alpine atmosphere with fine local cuisine.

Excursions

There is a post coach to **Meiringen** and **Rosenlaui** via the Grosse Scheidegg and the Schwarzwaldalp. Europe's most scenic gondola takes only half an hour to reach **First**, a difference in altitude of 3,300 feet (1,000m), accompanied all the way by an impressive Alpine panorama. An equally impressive gondola takes the visitor to **Männlichen**, while the Wengernalp railway goes to **Kleine Scheidegg** and **Wengernalp**. It is also from Grindelwald that one of the world's most famous rail journeys begins, first to Kleine Scheidegg and thence through the inside of the Eiger to the **Jungfraujoch**, from where you can enjoy an incomparable view of snow capped mountians. Particularly impressive are visits to the **upper Grindelwald glacier**, the **blue ice grotto**, and the **lower Grindelwald glacier**, with its romantic, narrow glacial gorge.

Tourist Office: Sportzentrum, CH-3818 Grindelwald (tel: (033) 854 1212)

◆◆◆ (summer)
◆◆◆ (winter)

GSTAAD

Although it has the reputation of being the resort of the 'jet set', this is only one side of Gstaad, and its range of hotels and amenities ensures that anyone can have an enjoyable stay here. One of Switzerland's most elegant resorts, it offers excellent facilities for both skier and non-skier, the surrounding 'white highland' region – including Saanen, Schönried and Rougemont – being superb. One pass covers the entire lift network, all local buses and trains between the resorts, plus entrance to Gstaad's heated indoor swimming pool.

Among this year-round resort's many other facilities are open air and indoor ice rinks for skating, plus one open air and four indoor rinks for curling (the Jackson Cup, the greatest curling prize in Europe is competed for at Gstaad); a three-mile (5km) toboggan run; sauna, massage and children's pool; indoor tennis and squash courts; plenty of paths for walkers; horses for hire and an indoor riding hall.

Hotels

The five-star **Palace Hotel** is everything a hotel of this standing should be, with attentive staff, excellent standards and good facilities. Also recommended are the **Bellevue Grand**, set in a delightful garden, and the charming **Landhaus**. More modest accommodation is rather more difficult to find.

Entertainment

There is an exceptional choice, ranging from sophisticated night spots to *Stüblis* where you can relax with a drink in a cosy atmosphere. Of special note is **La Cave**, in the basement of the **Hotel Olden**, while the **Greengo** at the Palace features internationally known bands. The **Chesery**, despite its vast dimensions, is also enjoyable.

Tourist Office: Hauptstrasse, CH-3780 Gstaad (tel: (033) 748 8181)

◆◆◆ (summer)
◆◆ (winter)
INTERLAKEN ✓

Set between the sparkling waters of Lake Thun (Thuner See) and Lake Brienz, (Brienzer See), Interlaken enjoys a magnificent setting on the banks of the River Aare.

One of Switzerland's longest-established holiday resorts, Interlaken lies in the heart of the country, in the Bernese Oberland, at an altitude of 1,864 feet (568m) and offers a wide range of facilities and amenities for sport, entertainment and excursions in the surrounding area. The **Jungfraujoch** and its famous railway station – the highest in Europe – or the **Schilthorn**, with its famous mountaintop revolving restaurant are just two possible trips.

With a capacity of some 4,500 beds, ranging from the modest guest house to the top luxury class grand hotel, the resort is well provided to meet the tastes and pockets of most visitors.

The main promenade, the **'Höheweg'** (known as the 'Höhe'), is lined with flowers and fronted by a huge open meadow from where you can enjoy one of the most famous views in the world with unimpeded vistas of snow-dusted mountains. Along the Höheweg are many of Interlaken's hotels, a selection of restaurants, tea rooms and

Enjoying a gentle stroll along Interlaken's restful Höheweg promenade

fashionable shops, not to mention the Kursaal Casino. Interlaken has large open-air and indoor heated swimming pools, a covered artificial ice rink and covered tennis courts, while in summer the nearby lakes offer opportunities for sailing, windsurfing, fishing and waterskiing as well as several lakeside beaches. Mini-golf, golf – there is an 18-hole lakeside course – and riding are also available.

Skiing

Interlaken's strategic location as gateway to the Bernese Oberland makes it a popular choice with those who do not mind not having a ski slope on their doorstep, but who use the lakeside resort as a base to visit different ski regions during the day.

Hotels

Combining an atmosphere of elegance, comfort and style, the **Hotel Beau Rivage**, on the Höheweg, is set in its own grounds by the River Aare, a few minutes' walk from Interlaken's centre. In the mid-price bracket, the **Beau-Site** at Seestrasse 16, also surrounded by its own gardens, is recommended. On the northside of the town, the Hirschen is a comfortable guesthouse run by the same family for nine generations.

Entertainment

There are a number of nightspots, discos, bars and cosy *Stüblis*, while each week in the winter usually sees a lively folklore evening. There is a night-club with live music, dancing and entertainment at the **Victoria-Jungfrau Hotel**, Höheweg 41; a popular pub at the **Hotel Splendid**, Höheweg 33; and typical rustic-style *Stüblis* at the **Hirschen** and **Kreuz** hotels.

In July and August there are romantic cruises with dancing on Lake Thun and special open-air performances in Interlaken itself of Schiller's drama *Wilhelm Tell*.

Restaurants

La Terrace at the Victoria-Jungfrau Hotel is the best in town. Also good is the **Hirschen**, and the **Pizzeria Piz Paz**, Bahnhofstrasse 1, the best pizza/pasta place in town. Afternoon tea at the **Café Schuh** is a 'must'.

Excursions

Lovely small villages are within easy access of Interlaken by means of the vintage steamers which ply the bigger, but shallower, of Interlaken's lakes, the Lake of Thun (Thuner See),

Train near Wengen: part of the spectacular mountain railway system

or by car or train along the shore. Among the most interesting are **Oberhofen**, noted for its medieval castle; **Spiez**, on the south shore of the lake, with an impressive castle and a fascinating museum; and **Thun**, at the far end of the lake, which also boasts a romantic castle as well as a museum.

Top of the list for most visitors is a trip on the **Jungfrau Railway**, for spectacular mountain scenery and the experience of actually passing through the Eiger mountain on the way to Jungfraujoch, Europe's highest railway station at 11,333 feet (3,454m). From the terrace of the Jungfraujoch Plateau there are fine views of the Aletchgletscher, the longest glacier in the Alps.

Tourist Office: Höheweg 37, CH-3800 Interlaken (tel: (033) 822 2121)

◆◆◆ (summer)
◆◆ (winter)
LUZERN (LUCERNE) ✓

Luzern may lack the cosmopolitanism of Zürich, Geneva or Bern, but it is surely the most delightful of Switzerland's cities, small enough to be walked round easily and with an excellent selection of hotels, restaurants, shops and sightseeing possibilities coupled with a magnificent setting.

Standing in the foothills of the St Gotthard Pass, Luzern borders the lake of the same name, which winds deep into the Alpine ranges of central Switzerland. Here, the gentle waterscape contrasts with wild, majestic scenery and, not surprisingly, lake excursions are high on the list of visitors' priorities.

The Lake Luzern Navigation company provides large, comfortable steamers and a range of half- or full-day excursions that can be combined with a trip to the top of a mountain. There are departures every hour, with a restaurant on board some services.

Sightseeing

Seeing the sights of Luzern on foot is a joy. You can stroll alongside the River Reuss, sample the delightful atmosphere, and marvel at the **Kapellbrücke** (Chapel Bridge), built in 1333, and recently restored after a fire. With its numerous gable paintings and sturdy water tower, it is the city's unmistakable landmark. Near by are quaint alleys and enchanting medieval buildings. In the city's arcades, on Tuesdays and Saturdays in particular, you can enjoy the hustle and bustle of the market crowd as you shop.

One of Switzerland's most popular museums is the **Verkehrshaus der Schweiz** (Swiss Transport Museum). Situated on the Luzern lakeside at Lidostrasse 5, the museum is reached from the centre of town by car, bus or ferryboat.

The museum traces the history, development and importance of transport on land, water and in the air and is one of the largest and most comprehensive collections of its kind in Europe.

Open: daily.

Hotels

The recently refurbished **Palace Hotel**, Haldenstrasse 10, dating from the end of the last century, is a delight, as are the 600 year old **Zum Rebstock** in the heart of the city at St Leodegarstrasse, and the **Grand Hotel National**, on the lakeshore at Haldenstrasse 4. In the moderate price bracket try the **Hotel Des Alpes** at Rathausquai 5.

Entertainment

Luzern boasts a wide range of sporting opportunities, from freshwater beaches to scenic golfing, with international horse-races, and rowing regattas on the Rotsee, traditional annual events.

By car it is only an hour to Engelberg, a superbly equipped winter sports area, while winter is also the season for Luzern's intriguing folk festival, *Fasnacht* or *Mardi Gras*.

Restaurants

Among the best in town are the **Schiff** in Unter der Egg, the **Old Swiss House**, Löwenplatz 4, and the **Barbatti**, which is located in a 19th-century building.

Excursions

The proud rock pyramid of **Mount Pilatus** is one of the chief landmarks of Luzern. The summit can be reached in two different ways. From Kriens (12 minutes by bus from Luzern), the four-seater cabins of a cablecar glide over fertile meadows and green forests to Fräkmüntegg. From there an aerial cableway – a daring feat of engineering – swings along

the steep cliff carrying visitors up to the peak, both in summer and winter.

From the end of April to the beginning of November the world-famous electric Pilatus railway climbs the mountain from Alpnachstad to Pilatus-Kulm. With a maximum gradient of 48°, this is the steepest cogwheel railway in the world. The way to Alpnachstad is along the shores of Lake Luzern by steamer, the Brünig railway, or by car.

The circular tour from Luzern-Alpnachstad up to Pilatus-Kulm and down to Kriens-Luzern is unforgettable. Among the many delightful small towns and

villages easily accessible from Luzern are **Zug**, standing on the shores of Lake Zug and set among orchards and gardens; **Gersau**, where laurels, chestnuts and fig trees grow in the mild climate; **Schwyz**, from which the country takes its name; **Hergiswil**, a pleasant, peaceful lakeside resort; and **Bürgenstock**, where numerous film stars and celebrities have homes.

Tourist Office: Frankenstrasse 1, CH-6002 Luzern (tel: (041) 410 7171)

Luzern's 14th-century Kapellbrücke with the even older Water Tower

◆◆◆ (summer)
◆◆ (winter)
MÜRREN
Set in a superb position on a mountain terrace facing the Jungfrau and the Eiger, Mürren has long been a popular choice with visitors, especially winter sports enthusiasts, even though the choice for skiing is not as great as in some of Switzerland's bigger resorts. It is traffic free as no roads lead to the resort, the village being reached, instead, either by funicular from Lauterbrunnen or by the 4-stage Schilthorn cable car from Stechelberg.
It is a very picturesque, unspoilt village which, with its wooden chalets and narrow winding alleys, has great charm and character. The Schilthorn towers above the resort and at its 10,000-foot (3,048m) summit there is a superb revolving restaurant which was featured in the James Bond film *On Her Majesty's Secret Service.*
There are easy nursery slopes in the centre of the village, and beginners are taken up to Allmendhubel with its gentle slopes and a drag lift to make things easier. There are special classes for children from three years of age.
Other sports facilities include an excellent leisure centre with indoor pool, whirlpool, squash courts, gymnasium, ice rink and a library, and there are also indoor tennis courts, a sauna and solarium, as well as a network of paths for walking.
A kindergarten for children under three is available in the mornings, and for children from three to six from 09.30 to

16.30hrs except Saturday and Sunday.

Hotels

The **Eiger** and the **Blumental** both enjoy excellent reputations. The **Hotel Alpina** is a family-run guest house whose restaurant enjoys an unrivalled view.

Tourist Office: Sportzentrum, CH-3825 Mürren (tel: (033) 856 8686)

◆◆ (summer)
◆ (winter)
WEGGIS

This little resort with its flower-decked promenades, lakeside lido and mild, sunny climate, is about 40 minutes by lake steamer from Luzern.
A good spot for a relaxing break, Weggis offers a variety of excellent leisure facilities including a heated indoor swimming pool, outdoor tennis courts, fishing, sailing and windsurfing. Each morning in the high season you can enjoy a concert on the lakeside bandstand or in one of the hotels. There are numerous walks in the hills behind Weggis and there are concerts and folklore evenings throughout the summer. The 'Rose Festival', hosted each year by Weggis and including music, dancing and a fireworks display, takes place the last weekend in June.

Hotels

Set in beautiful grounds which provide flowers for the hotel and fresh fruit and vegetables for the kitchen, the **Park Hotel** enjoys a quiet, lakeside location.

Tourist Office: CH-6353 Weggis (tel: (041) 390 1155)

◆◆◆ (summer)
◆◆◆ (winter)
WENGEN

Wengen is a perfect place for relaxing and unwinding – there is very little to disturb the peace, not even a road up from the Lauterbrunnen valley. Instead, everyone and everything comes here by the mountain railway which continues on up to Kleine Scheidegg and the Jungfraujoch and which also links Wengen with Grindelwald.
The resort's real advantage is the direct access to the whole Jungfrau region, by means of

either the mountain railway to Wengernalp or the cable car to the top of the Männlichen from where there is an enormous choice of runs.

In summer this friendly resort offers many walks around the village, along a network of paths which take you through mountain woods and flower-filled meadows with views of the Jungfrau Glacier and over the valley to the Schilthorn.

Hotels

The 5-star **Park Hotel Beausite** enjoys a peaceful location set back from the village centre with

The quiet little resort of Wengen is a gateway to the Jungfrau region

beautiful views of the Jungfrau range, and offers traditional Swiss hospitality in luxurious surroundings – including an indoor pool. The **Falken** is a superb old museum on the fringe of the village.

Entertainment

You will not find the sophistication or the choice of St Moritz or Davos here, but there is still plenty to do in the evenings. Both the **Pickel Bar** and the **Tanne Stübli** are popular, and usually packed;

and the **Arvenstube** offers a good atmosphere, often with an accordianist playing. Also excellent is the **Figgeller Bar** on the practice slope.

The **Silberhornstube** is another spot with a casual, relaxed atmosphere and live music. For a lively evening with music you could try **The Pub** nightspot or **Tiffany's Disco**. The **Carousel** has a live group and a more sophisticated atmosphere.

Tourist Office: CH-3823 Wengen (tel: (033) 855 1414)

◆◆◆ (summer)
◆◆ (winter)

WILDERSWIL

This is a picture-postcard village with its traditional old chalets decked in summer with pink and red pelargoniums, its green fields and meadows and beautiful panoramic views.

The village is an ideal starting point for easy walks through the meadows and on the lower mountain slopes.

Not to be missed is a trip on the rack-and-pinion railway which leads up from Wilderswil to the

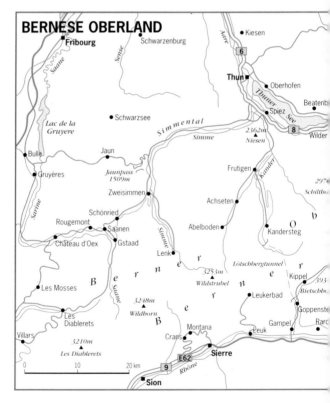

BERNESE OBERLAND

famous **Alpine Garden** at
Schynige Platte.

Hotels

The **Hotel Schlössli** is a little
chalet-style hotel set in an idyllic
location on the edge of
Wilderswil village. The **Victoria**
is a better bet for families.

Tourist Office: Lehngasse, CH-
3812 (tel: (033) 822 8455)

*A popular excursion from Wilderswil
is to the Schynige Platte, with its
views and Alpine Garden*

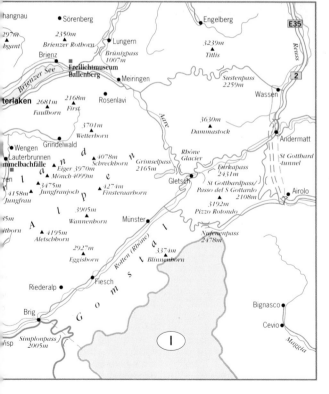

THE GRISONS (GRAUBUNDEN)

The largest of Switzerland's cantons, covering about a sixth of the country's land mass, the Grisons is also the only one where three languages – German, Italian and Romansch – are spoken. It comprises remote farms and villages and numerous popular holiday resorts such as glitzy St Moritz, Davos, Flims and Klosters. Capital of the Grisons is the ancient cathedral city of Chur.

◆◆ (summer)
◆◆◆ (winter)
AROSA
This long-established and popular resort is an attractive and lively village remotely set in superb scenery at the head of the spectacular Plessur Valley. A resort that combines much of the sophistication of St Moritz with the casual, relaxed atmosphere of many smaller Swiss resorts, Arosa has accommodation ranging from five-star de luxe hotels to small family *pensions*.

For winter sports enthusiasts, however, there are varied slopes and, although there are no very difficult runs for the really expert skier, there is plenty to satisfy the intermediate or good skier. All the ski areas are interconnecting and form a well-planned and efficient network with over 45 miles (72km) of downhill runs which are prepared and patrolled. *Langlauf* (cross-country skiing) is popular with visitors to Arosa, and there are nearly 20 miles (32km) of special pistes.

Other resort facilities include a toboggan run, two natural ice-skating rinks and two artificial rinks, tennis and squash facilities, horse-riding, bowling alleys and a casino, as well as paths for walking.

At the **Park Hotel** a kindergarten operates from 09.00 to 18.00hrs Monday to Friday, free of charge to hotel guests.

Hotels
The **Arosa Kulm Hotel** is located in a prime position in inner Arosa and offers a good range of facilities. The **Waldhotel-National** is situated in its own park amid pine woods, a few minutes' walk from the village. The old-fashioned **Belri**, opposite the museum, has plenty of character.

Entertainment
This ranges from the casual to the sophisticated. There is a casino with gaming room and a smart disco bar. Other Arosa nightspots include the **Crazy-Nightclub** in the Posthotel, **Strapspub** at the Beau-Rivage and the **Cheminée-Bar** at the Hotel Arve Central. The **Los** is an excellent café-bar. The **Tschuggen** and **Kulm** both have smart nightspots. From time to time there are ice galas and ice hockey matches, while the horse-races on snow are one of the highlights of the season.

Restaurants
Among the best restaurants are the **Roggenmoser** at the Hotel Eden and the **Bajazzo**, with its Italian menu. The **Bündneikeller** at the Hotel Bellevue and the **Bündnerstubbe** at the

Tschuggen specialise in fondue. During après-ski the place to be seen is the **Kaiser** tearoom.

Excursion

The 20-minute cable car journey to the top of **Weisshorn** at 8,704 feet (2,653m) is rewarded by the magnificent panorama of the snowy ridges of the Grisons Alps.

Tourist Office: CH-7050 Arosa (tel: (081) 378 7020)

◆◆ (summer)
◆◆ (winter)
CHUR

Chur (pronounced 'Koor') is still a major junction and many never get beyond the railway station – which is a pity because there is much to see, and 'doing

Winter view of Arosa, sheltered in its hollow, across the ski slopes

the sights' here is made simple by red and green footprints which lead you through the town's nooks and crannies right to the historic places. However, care should be taken in following the trails, as the markings are so unobtrusive that it is easy to lose your way. The red trail takes you first to the 15th-century Gothic **Rathaus** (town hall), and eventually to the **Rhätisches Museum** (Rhaetic Museum), taking in various sights on the way.

The green path leads you to the Plessur, a tributary of the Rhein, and to the **Upper Gate**.
The **Bischöflicher Schloss**

49

(Bishop's Palace) and the **Cathedral of Our Lady** are quickly reached by following the steps through the tower gate. The cathedral impresses with its sheer massiveness, while the cathedral, treasury bears witness to the centuries-old religious heritage of the city. Also of interest are:

The **Bünder Kunstmuseum** (Fine Arts Museum) in Postplatz, with important works by Swiss artists among others.

Open: daily except Mondays.

A private **carriage collection** from the 19th century, in the Romantik Hotel Stern.

Open: daily.

Hotels

The **Romantik Hotel Stern**, Reichgasse 11, occupying a 17th-century building with rustic décor, is very good.

Restaurants

Excellent food can be enjoyed in the restaurant of the **Rebleuten Hotel**, and at **Zum Alten Zollhaus**, occupying part of the former customs house. Among the many prosperous and convivial inns, the **Drei Könige** is noteworthy.

Excursions

Chur is an excursion hub. The narrow-gauge Rhaetian Railway is a fun way of visiting **Arosa** and the **Engadine**, **Davos** or **Disentis** with its Benedictine monastery in baroque style. The yellow coaches of the Swiss Alpine Post will carry you to **Lenzerheide**, **St Moritz**, or **Flims**; or over the **Splügen Pass** and **San Bernardino** to the **Ticino**.

Tourist Office: Grabenstrasse 5/PF 766, CH-7002 Chur (tel: (081) 252 1818)

◆◆ (summer)
◆◆◆ (winter)

DAVOS

Davos is one of Switzerland's premier ski resorts, providing some of the best winter skiing in the world, with a fine lift system, reliable snow conditions and a host of après-ski facilities. Located in a peaceful Alpine valley, it is divided into two parts – **Platz** and **Dorf** – (but without any clear distinction between the two) and is a lively, if architecturally undistinguished place with a number of charming restaurants, cafés and stylish boutiques. It has a long history as a health resort, and was famously patronised by Robert Louis Stevenson and Sir Arthur Conan-Doyle amongst other 19th-century notables. With 12,000 inhabitants, Davos is even larger than St Moritz, offering 17 hotels with 6,500 beds during the winter season, and in summer 4,600 beds in hotels and boarding houses. About 10,000 beds in rented apartments and private rooms are available all year.

Winter Sports

Davos is the largest ski resort of the Grisons. The ski slopes that attract the crowds are on the sides of the Strela chain of mountains, dominated by the Weissfluhjoch. The **Parsenn funicular railway** gives access to the most remarkable snow fields in the country, taking skiers from Davos up to Weissfluhjoch, nearly 9,000 feet (2,750m) high, and the top of the Parsenn run.

From there they can ski down 3,500 feet (1,000m) to the town, or, take a northwesterly route to reach the neighbouring resort of **Klosters** (see ► 53).

Another funicular, combined with a gondola, goes to **Strela** and, by a junction line, to the **Parsenn** area. On the left side of the Davos Valley is the well-equipped **Brämabüel – Jakobshorn** ski area, reached by cable car and skilifts. **Pischa**, a ski station situated in the Flüela Valley and reached by bus from Davos-Dorf, offers ski runs situated on the south and sunny face of the mountain.

In **Glaris**, just to the south of Davos, is a chairlift to the **Rinerhorn** (7,500 feet/2,200m). Over 50 miles (80km) of cross-country ski tracks are well prepared. Ski instructors of the Swiss Ski School teach children and adults in downhill skiing and cross-country skiing; and special weekly arrangements known as White Weeks, combining skiing and/or cross-country skiing are popular in December, January and April.

Summer Facilities

In summer Davos is equally delightful. It has 200 miles (320km) of well-kept walks and paths through town, mountains and forest; climbing and mountaineering weeks are organised; and the resort offers sailing, windsurfing, swimming in the Lake of Davos or the open

Davos makes an equally attractive base in summer and winter

air and indoor swimming pools, trout fishing in either the lake or the Landwasser River and its tributaries, golf on an 18-hole course, horseback riding and tennis.

A children's playground is set in the middle of town, and there are numerous picnic places in the surroundings.

Walks

A walk (one hour there and back) can be made along the **Hohe Promenade**, a perfectly planned walk, level, sometimes under trees, and kept clear of snow in winter. It may be reached from Davos-Dorf from near the Parsenn funicular station or from Davos-Platz by a steep path leading up to the Catholic church.

The countryside around Davos provides endless walking possibilities through meadows, past farms and up into the mountains with magnificent views all around. For a more leisurely ascent to the peak, a variety of cable cars and funiculars is available from mid-June, taking visitors up to **Jakobshorn** at 8,500 feet (2,600m) or the **Parsenn** at 9,200 feet (2,800m), while the five-minute funicular ride up to **Schatzalp** should not be missed. You can visit the **Alpine Flower Garden** and return on foot through the pine woods with squirrels at practically every bend.

Hotels and Restaurants

The **Steigenberger Belvedere** is a 'grand' hotel in the true sense of the word, and enjoys a superb situation with views over the valley towards the

Jakobshorn. Also recommended is the **Central Sporthotel**, noted for its attentive service. The **Hotel Edelweiss** offers simple, family accommodation in Davos-Dorf. Notable restaurants include the **Bündnerstübli**, Dischmastrasse 8, Davos Dorf, and the reasonably priced **Grand Café** in Davos Platz. For an excellent fondue try the **Gentiana** – and for delicious pastries and hot chocolate either the **Café Fah** or **Schneider's**.

Entertainment

Popular spots are the **Postli Club** with top groups and showbands and the **Montana**, with live music and dancing. The younger crowd favour the **Café Carlos**, the **Express Bar** and the **Cabana**, while for a real Swiss atmosphere with folklore there is the popular **Cava Grischa**.

Tourist Office: Promenade 67, Davos Platz, CH-7270 Davos (tel: (081) 415 2121).

◆◆ (summer)
◆◆ (winter)

FLIMS

Flims ranks among the best-known tourist resorts of the Grisons. It is set on a terrace above the Rhein gorge amid spectacular scenery and, although considerably extended in recent years, it is still essentially a village resort – in fact two villages: **Flims-Dorf,** the traditional residential section and **Flims-Waldhaus**, whose hotels are scattered through a forest of conifers. The nearby village of **Laax** also shares the same ski area, known as 'the white arena'.

The splendid setting is perhaps Flims's greatest attraction

Among Flims's many facilities are cross-country ski trails including a two-mile (3km) piste which is illuminated at night three times a week, many footpaths (open winter and summer) and a toboggan run. There is an indoor ice skating rink at the sports centre together with four indoor rinks for curling, and several hotels have swimming pools.

Hotels

Among the best is the **Parkhotel Waldhaus**, situated in its own estate on the edge of the village, while **Hotel National** is a pleasant small family hotel in Waldhaus.

Entertainment

This is lively and varies from sophisticated to casual. The **Crap Ner Hotel** in Dorf has a live band and is popular with groups, while the **Stenna Bar**, opposite the cable car in Flims Dorf, appeals to the younger set. The **Caverna** is an old wine cellar with a superb ambience.

Tourist Office: CH-7018 Flims (tel: (081) 920 9202)

◆◆ (summer)
◆◆◆ (winter)
KLOSTERS

Three decades of popularity with royalty, film stars and the jet-set have not spoiled Klosters. Nestled beneath a sparkle of snow-covered peaks, this fairytale village comes complete with horse-drawn sleighs, friendly countryfolk and a cluster of picturesque chalets. Skiers have the choice of 24 mountain railways and skilifts, all within a stone's throw of the village. Of the numerous ski runs in the **Gotschna/Parsenn** area, the favourite is still the descent from the top of the **Weissfluh** down to **Küblis**. The return ride from Küblis to Klosters is included in the Klosters/Davos regional ski pass which also provides access to skiing on the **Madrisa** and in the **Pischa**, **Jakobshorn** and **Rinerhorn** areas shared with neighbouring Davos. The Madrisa cable car opens up an extensive area of intermediate skiing served by five lifts. Cross-country skiers have for many years sung the praises of Klosters.

More than 25 scenic miles (40km) of varied trails are prepared daily. Nor are walkers forgotten with a choice of well-prepared, clearly marked paths ranging from gentle walks near the village to more challenging itineraries on the **Madrisa** or up to **Alp Garfiun**.

And for those who prefer a 'holiday on ice', Klosters offers curling at the Hotel Parsenn and skating on the two natural rinks at the resort's sports ground.

Hotels

The exclusive **Hotel Pardenn** is expensive but recommended, as is the small – only 11 rooms – but very smart **Walserhof Hotel**.

Restaurants

The restaurant of the **Walserhof** is as good as the hotel, and also to be recommended are the **Alte Post** and the unpretentious **Höhwald**.

Tourist Office: Alte Bahnhofstrasse, CH-7250 Klosters (tel: (081) 410 2020)

◆◆◆ (summer)
◆◆◆ (winter)
ST MORITZ ✓

St Moritz, located on the southern side of the Alps at an altitude of 6,000 feet (1,800m) above sea-level, remains one of Switzerland's best-known and best-loved resorts, especially with the prosperous. Its first visitors came for the healing mineral springs which were discovered as long ago as the Bronze Age. Winter guests have been coming since 1864.

St Moritz-Dorf lies half-way up the slope at the foot of the leaning campanile (**Schiefer Turm**), the only vestige of the original village, and is bristling with palatial hotels. **St Moritz Bad** is the spa quarter, its extensive installations spreading around the lake.

The town is the birthplace of winter tourism and modern winter sports in the Alps, and is Switzerland's only Olympic host resort.

The high probability of snow and good weather, thanks to the high altitude and southern exposure, ensures a long winter season, with visitors attracted by the possibilities for downhill and cross-country skiing and other attractions such as the Cresta bob run.

Being at the heart of the Engadine region, winter skiers have access to superb, varied skiing. The most celebrated of the five local ski areas is the **Corvatsch**. Here snow is virtually guaranteed (the upper slopes are also used for summer skiing) and conditions are ideal for late-season skiing. In summer, the chief appeal of St Moritz lies in the wide range of sports facilities available, such as summer skiing, sailing, windsurfing, tennis, horseback riding, golf on the highest and oldest 18-hole golf course in continental Europe, ice-skating and other activities, all found within a 20-minute driving radius.

The stunning Upper Engadine landscape with its 25 mountain lakes, four of which are ideal for sailing and windsurfing, all add to the attractions, as do the health spa, the numerous cultural programmes, and the **Swiss National Park**, within an hour's drive.

St Moritz is Switzerland's most chic resort, especially in winter

Pontresina

Pontresina is a small village resort with buildings in the typical Engadine painted style, which lies in a sheltered valley at 6,000 feet (1,800m) just ten minutes by train from St Moritz and sharing the same ski area. It is much less sophisticated than St Moritz, but is a charming resort nevertheless – and much cheaper and friendlier than its neighbour!

Hotels and Restaurants

The well-heeled visitor to St Moritz is spoiled for choice of excellent hotels, the **Carlton**, **Badrutt's Palace** and **Suvretta House** being among the best. The moderately priced **Soldanella** is also recommended. Of the numerous excellent restaurants,

the most fashionable include **Chesa Veglia**; the **Rôtisserie des Chevaliers** at the **Kulm Hotel**; and **Crystal's Grissini**. In Pontresina, **Pension Edelweiss** is a charming chalet-style hotel offering inexpensive accommodation.

Entertainment

The entertainment available in St Moritz is wide ranging, with horse-racing on the frozen lake in January and February, a casino, fashion shows, night-clubs, discos, cafés, cinemas, concerts, galas and competitions.

Tourist Office: via Maistra 12, CH-7500 St Moritz (tel: (081) 837 3333)

SOUTHERN SWITZERLAND

This region is the location of the Italian-speaking Ticino region, with its delightful lakeland areas and resorts such as Locarno and Lugano. It is also home of the area known as the Valais (Wallis in German), with the mighty River Rhône at its core and bounded by some of the highest peaks in the Alps. It is here that one finds some of Switzerland's most attractive sports resorts, including Crans/Montana, Saas-Fee, Verbier and Zermatt.

◆◆◆ (summer)
◆◆ (winter)

ASCONA

Situated in a picturesque bay on Lake Maggiore, close to Locarno, Ascona owes its fame to artists. Exhibitions in the cultural Centre and the Museum for Modern Art, countless galleries and antique shops, readings and lectures, bear witness to its active cultural life. Giovanni Serodine, arguably the most talented painter from the Ticino, lived here in the 17th century. Three of his paintings are hung in the church of **Santi Pietro e Paolo**.

The **Collegio Pontificio Papio** was endowed in the 16th century by Bartolemeo Papio, a native of Ascona. The former sanctuary today serves as a secondary school. Its splendid renaissance court is decorated with the coats of arms of sponsors and protectors over a period of five centuries. **Santa Maria della Misericordia**, a church attached to the college, contains valuable frescos.

Palm trees nod to snowy peaks across Lake Maggiore at Ascona

Ascona caters for its guests in 50 hotels with a total of 3,100 beds, and a further 5,400 in holiday apartments and private accommodation. There is an underground car park in the centre and further parking facilities by the lake and on entering the town.

Hotels and Restaurants
Amongst a wide choice of luxury hotels, the 5 star **Giardino** on the fringe of town stands out. At the budget end, the **Riposo** has a rooftop swimming pool. The **Ristorante degli Angioli** serves Ticino cuisine in a delightful setting.

Sports and Entertainment
Ascona has a wide range of sports and entertainment to offer its guests: riding, golf, tennis, squash, swimming, windsurfing, sailing and waterskiing, as well as an ice rink for skating and curling. Attractive, well-maintained paths for walking and hiking open up the area round the town, and there is also a fitness track and a cycling path from Ascona to Bellinzona, which follows the lake for some distance but also passes through the fields in the Magadino plain. Drawing courses are offered regularly, both in hotels and in the open air, and courses in bookbinding are also available.

Culture
For more than 40 years the annual international music festival, held from August to October, has presented classical concerts with world-famous conductors, orchestras and soloists. Another major attraction is the New Orleans

Jazz Festival, lasting 10 days in June and July, when Ascona's picturesque squares and alleys take on a particularly lively and colourful atmosphere.

Excursions
To get a feel of the countryside you should visit **Ronco**, a picturesque village set a short distance to the west, high above Lake Maggiore. The isolated valleys above Ronco are worth exploring. The most rustic, **Val Verzasca**, can be reached by car or postbus.

Tourist Office: Casa Serodine, viale Papio, CH-6612 Ascona (tel: (091) 791 0090)

◆◆ (summer)
◆ (winter)

BELLINZONA
The capital city of the Ticino is an important industrial centre and rail transport hub, being located half-way between the fruitful Lombard Plain of Italy and the rugged Swiss Alps. The town has much to interest and fascinate, not least three castles and the ancient city walls. The oldest and largest of the castles, is the **Castello Grande** (or **Castle of Uri**), first mentioned in documents of the 6th century. The immense courtyard, which can be visited, was used in times of crisis as a refuge by the entire population. Steep walkways lead from the old city to the castle's heights. The ancient walls have been well preserved and still link Castello Grande and its counterpart **Castello di Montebello** (or **Schwyz**). This castle originated in the late 13th or early 14th century and was subsequently

destroyed and restored on numerous occasions. Its main tower and *palazzetto* encompass a small museum featuring both history and archaeology.
Open: daily except Mondays.
High above the city is the **Castello di Sasso Corbaro**, (or **Unterwalden**), built in 1479 in just six months. Several rooms in its tower are dedicated to a collection of folk art and folklore.
Open: daily except Mondays, April–October.
Bellinzona's three forts are still referred to as the castles of **Uri**, **Schwyz** and **Unterwald**.
The old city down below has elegant façades of patrician houses, ornamental iron balconies and gateways, rococo portals and fine inn signs.

Hotels
The **Hotel Unione**, via GL-Guisan, is a simple hotel, set in delightful gardens. The **San Giovanni** provides good, plain accommodation.

Excursions
A trip by car or postbus leads into the lonely yet enchanting **Valle Morobbia** and its chestnut forests. The sunny terrace of **Mornera**, a rewarding vantage point for the areas, can be reached by aerial cableway. Not to be missed is the '**Climbing Garden**' at **Molinazzo**.

Tourist Office: Palazzo Civico, via Camminata (tel: (081) 825 2131)

◆◆ (summer)
◆◆◆ (winter)
CRANS-MONTANA
At the heart of the Alps a large plateau, covered with pine forests and scattered lakes, faces the highest mountains of

The formidably defended Castello Grande at Bellinzona

Europe – from the Matterhorn to Mont Blanc. Set on this sunny plateau at 5,000 feet (1,500km), with a spectacular view of the Rhône valley, are the adjoining villages of Crans (Crans-sur-Sierre to give it its full name) and Montana.

In summer, there are many delightful walks through beautiful mountain scenery, following the lakeside or crossing the mountainside through forests. Cable cars take you up to 10,000 feet (3,000m) for even more spectacular scenery and views across the Valais from the many belvederes. For instance, a cable car from Crans makes a magnificent ascent over the Rhône valley to **Bella Lui** at 8,340 feet (2,543m).

The resort offers summer visitors any number of leisure activities. You can enjoy the facilities of the new sports and leisure complex, sunbathe and swim on the shores of **Lake Moubra**, play golf on what must be one of the most panoramic golf courses in the Alps, try your skills at ice-skating on the artificial ice rink, go riding, or play tennis.

As a winter resort, Crans-Montana has gained in popularity in recent years and is now one of the leading resorts in Switzerland, with an excellent record for snow, plenty of ski runs to appeal to both the beginner and the intermediate skier, and nearly 100 miles (160km) of prepared pistes.

Hotels

The **Hotel Crans Ambassador** enjoys an enviable position just above Montana with lovely panoramic views over Lake Grenon and towards the mountains. It is rivalled for views by the more moderately priced **Mont-Blanc**.

Entertainment

In Crans, The **George and Dragon** pub is a lively and popular bar; **Dancing Nightclub Absolut** is more sophisticated; and the **Sporting Club** is a select nightspot with live music, dancing and a gaming room. Montana has **Madisson**, with an orchestra, dancing and cabaret, while **Number Two** is a karaoke bar.

Excursions

Interesting excursions are possible to the traffic-free resort of **Zermatt** or the magnificent **Val d'Anniviers** and the picturesque villages of **Zinal** and **Grimentz**.

Tourist Office: CH-3962 Crans-Montana (tel: (027) 485 0444)

◆◆◆ (summer)
◆ (winter)

LOCARNO

On the shores of Lake Maggiore, Locarno is a combination of resort and business centre. It has its old town where patrician houses look simple on the outside yet are magnificent inside, with old and cosy streets so narrow one can touch the walls of the opposite houses by stretching one's arms. And there is modern Locarno with department stores, wide avenues and all the up-to-date facilities of a tourist resort. The town boasts many historical sights. **Madonna del Sasso**, the pilgrimage church, is Locarno's emblem, reached by funicular

The pilgrimage church of Madonna del Sasso, on a crag above Locarno

from Contrada Cappuccini. The **Castello Visconti** (also known as **Rusca**) once served as a fortress and was the largest of its kind in Ticino; today it houses the **archaeological museum** with its rich collection of local prehistoric and Roman finds. *Open*: daily except Mondays. Locarno's churches are well worth a visit: **Sant' Antonio**, with its magnificent marble altars; **Chiesa Nuova**, with its stucco ceiling and relics; **San Vittore**, one of the major Romanesque sacred buildings in the Ticino; and **Santa Maria in Selva**, which has fine 15th-century frescos.

Culture

Locarno's International Film Festival held every August is one of the main cultural events in the Ticino, and the music festival held from May to July has become a popular meeting place for music-lovers.

Facilities

Locarno has been busy adding to its visitor facilities, increasing the number of open air swimming pools and improving its tennis courts located along the lake. Watersports are also available, and there is an 18-hole golf course only five minutes away by car. For the more adventurous there are courses in parachuting and para-gliding. Along the lakeshore promenade, subtropical trees, shrubs and flowers have been planted and are lovingly cared for.

Hotels and Restaurants

The **Palma au Lac** is a lovely place with a deservedly high reputation. Also recommended are the first-class **Reber au Lac** and **Grand Hotel** and, among the moderately priced establishments, the **Beau Rivage**, many of whose rooms face the lake, and which has an *al fresco* restaurant in summer. Of the many good restaurants the **Panorama at the Dellaville Hotel**, **Centenario** and **Coq d'Or** are among the best – the **Citadella**, located in a centuries-old house in the old part of town, has a particularly good atmosphere.

Excursions

Locarno is ideally placed as an excursion centre for the magnificent **Ticino Valleys** stretching north to the **Leopontine Alps**. The **Valle Maggia**, and its tributary **Val Barona**, are amongst the most beautiful.

The town is also the main embarkation point for steamship trips on **Lake Maggiore**, most unforgettably to the spellbinding subtropical paradise of the **Isles of Brissago**.

Tourist Office: Largo Zorzi CH-6601 Locarno (tel: (091) 751 0333)

◆◆◆ (summer)
◆ (winter)

LUGANO

Set between Monte Brè and Monte San Salvatore, Lake Lugano shimmers with light and colour, offering the visitor a sunny climate and a warm, lively atmosphere.

Lugano has preserved its fascinating traffic-free historic centre and is host to two of the most famous churches in Ticino: **San Lorenzo** and **St Mary of the Angels**.

Gardens and promenades fringe the lakeside from **Paradiso** towards **Castagnola**, from where a footpath continues to **Gandria**, one of the Ticino's most picturesque villages, which can also be reached by lake steamer.

The **Villa Favorita**, on the lake front at Castagnola, still houses some of the Thyssen-Bornemisza collection and has regular exhibitions from the rest of the collection (now in Madrid).

The resort has two principal lidos for sunbathing and swimming; and waterskiing, windsurfing and sailing are also available. The less energetic may prefer to enjoy the scenery from one of the steamers which call regularly, or relax in one of the many pavement cafés and enjoy a cool drink while listening to one of the concerts which are frequently held in the piazza della Riformo or the lakeside gardens.

Hotels and Restaurants

The two most imposing hotels, both overlooking the lake, are the **Grand Hotel Eden** and the **Splendide Royale**. The most voguish is the elegant **Villa Principe Leopoldo**. Also recommended is the moderately priced **Hotel Ticino**, piazza Cioccara 1, set in a centuries-old house and refurbished in Città-Vecchia period style. One of the best restaurants in town is **Al Portone** in viole Casserate. Also excellent are **Cyrano**, corso Pestalozzi 27, and **Santabbondio** in Sorengo, about 3km to the southwest of Lugano.

Entertainment
In the evenings, visitors have the choice between local bars, restaurants or sophisticated nightspots. Alternatively, a quiet stroll along the waterfront or an evening cruise with music may be more appealing.
The concert season runs from April to June followed by the lake festival at the end of July. The **Vintage Parade**, held on the first Sunday in October, is an event when the whole town comes together to have a good time.

Excursions
Just south of Lugano, near the valley of Morcote, **Swissminiatur** (Switzerland in Miniature) presents scale models of Swiss landmarks, including working models of trains and cable cars.

Lugano enjoys a pleasant lakeside setting and mild climate

Open: daily from mid-March to October.

Tourist Office: Palazzo Civico, CH-6901 Lugano (tel: (091) 921 4664)

◆◆◆ (summer)
◆◆ (winter)
THE GOMS VALLEY
Also known as the Conches Valley, or Upper Rhône Valley, this lateral 30 mile (48km) trench climbs west to east from the old trading centre of Brig to the high-lying glacier town of Gletsch. Scenery of increasing grandeur unfolds at every stage of this upward climb, and each new village appears to surpass its lower neighbour in charm and character. At Morel, five miles (7.5km) east of Brig, a cable-car ascends to the small but beautifully sited resort of Riederalp lying at a height of nearly 7,500 feet (2,230 metres). A short distance from Morel is another lift to the summit of Moosfluh which provides a splendid view of the lower reaches of the Aletsch Glacier, the largest in Switzerland which starts its 17 mile (27km) descent from the south side of the Jungfrau massif. Rivalling Riederalp for location is the similarly sited mountain resort of Bettmeralp further east. Just before Fiesch, further along the valley, there is a road leading south of the charming old village of Ernen – well worth a detour. From Ernen a winding road climbs up the pastoral Binn valley to the remote and beautiful hamlets of Binn and Im Feld. From Fiesch itself there is another cable-car climbing in two stages to the Eggishorn, which at

an altitude of nearly 10,000 feet (3,000 metres) affords one of the finest views in the Valais. The Aletsch glacier sweeps down to the west, and to the east the Fiesch glacier appears poised to roll down onto the small hamlets beneath it. The next village of significance is Bellwald, reached either by narrow road or cable way two miles (3km) from Fiesch. An attractive huddle of typical larchwood chalets, it is surrounded to the north by a number of tiny hamlets each distinguished by ancient Alpine chapels. The view south from Bellwald is worth the diversion. The village of Niederwald, notable for its picturesque collection of traditional timber houses, has earned modest fame as the birthplace of Cesar Ritz – the renowned hotelier whose name is now synonymous with luxurious surroundings. Reckingen, straddling the road ahead, is notable for its handsome 18th-century baroque church complete with macabre glass-encased robed skeletons. The principal community of the Goms, Munster, lies beyond after which the valley becomes wilder and more mountainous. After the little village of Oberwald, the valley twists tortuously past the Rhône Falls until the canton border town of Gletsch with its electrifying view of the famous Rhône Glacier above.

Hotels

The main accommodation centres of the valley are at Riederalp and Bettmeralp. Recommended hotels in the former include the 4 star **Art Furrer** and the more modestly priced **Bergdohle**. A

good value place in Bettmeralp is the **Alpfrieden**.

Tourist Office: CH-3981 Riederalp (tel: (027) 927 1365)
Tourist Office: CH-3992 Bettmeralp (tel: (027) 927 1291)

◆◆ (summer)
◆◆◆ (winter)
SAAS-FEE

The charming village of Saas-Fee in the canton of Valais lies among magnificent mountains and glaciers in the heart of the highest Swiss Alps. No cars are allowed in the village itself, but transport is provided by horse-drawn sleigh or small electrically powered vehicles operated by the local taxi service as well as many hotels. One of the services offered by the Tourist Office, located near the bus station at the entrance to the village, is an electronic system which allows visitors to notify the hotel of their arrival; a hotel porter will then arrive with an electric car to transport the guests and their luggage.

The village of Saas-Fee has retained its Alpine flavour. Weather-beaten chalets and clusters of ancient barns are protected by the community, but some have been modernised to offer comfortable accommodation and shops. The 'Pearl of the Alps', as Saas-Fee is known, is surrounded by 13 lofty mountains. The Dom, 14,912 feet (4,545m) is the highest mountain completely within Swiss territory.

For winter skiers, it is one of the best resorts in Switzerland. The

63

Restaurant overlooking Saas-Fee

learner will find gentle slopes at the base of the mountain, while the enthusiast will delight in the black and red runs over the glaciers which run from three sides down into the valley. The 'Metro Alpin' (installed in 1984) is the world's highest underground funicular, running from Felskinn to Mittelallin. It takes skiers up to 11,500 feet (3,500m) where, of course, snow is always guaranteed. Summer mountaineering continues to be of prime importance and the resort employs 40 guides in its mountaineering school. Programmes offered vary from easy tours to challenging climbs to the highest peaks. There are also ski-touring weeks in the spring and hiking weeks in the autumn.

Other facilities include tennis courts, a tennis school, public swimming pool with children's pool and sauna, miniature golf, horse riding and bowling. Children aged three to six can be cared for in a kindergarten located in the village and supervised by a nurse.

Hotels and Restaurants

Saas-Fee has close to 7,500 beds in its 45 hotels and 1,300 chalets and apartments offering good standards of cleanliness, comfort and hospitality. Among the best are the **Metropol Grand Hotel** and the **Romantik Hotel Beau-Site**. Over 60 restaurants feature varied menus and friendly service, that at the **Waldhotel Fletschhorn** being outstanding.

Entertainment

The **Metropol Nightlife** at the **Metropol Grand Hotel** has a live group and a good atmosphere, while **Popcorn**, with its rustic décor, is also a popular dancing spot. The **Sissy**, **Nesti's**, and the **Go-Inn** are similarly energetic venues.

Excursions

Daily excursions are operated to various resorts such as **Zermatt** and **Chamonix**, while on the Felskinn visitors can see an **ice grotto** through an ice tunnel extending 200 feet (60m).

Tourist Office: CH-3906 Saas-Fee (tel: (027) 322 8586)

◆◆ (summer)
◆ (winter)

SION

The impression gained on approaching Sion is one of grandeur, the castle ruins of Tourbillon and its twin fortress-church Valère bestowing a

Sion with its twin fortified crags

sense of durability on the capital of the Valais, and emphasising its strong natural defensive position.

Signs of the Past

In 1961, at the edge of the River Sitter's erosion cone, in the 'Petit Chasseur', archaeologists discovered the earliest known evidence of Sion's settlement: one of the most important Neolithic (3000–1500BC) sites to be unearthed in Alpine regions. In the schoolyard of the Secondary School for Girls, several Stone Age monuments have been recovered, including dolmens, graves and monoliths.

Old Sion

The orange-coloured **Town Hall** is a magnificent building of the 17th century, with a domed tower, rich woodcarvings and wrought-iron embellishments. The latter are even more delicately executed on the houses of the nobility that extend along Grand Pont and through its sidestreets. Hemmed in by the rue de Conthey and the rue de Lausanne is the most elegant building in the Valais, the **Maison Supersaxo**, built during the Renaissance but late

Gothic in appearance.
Leaving the centre of the city along the Grand Pont, the visitor should roam through the old sector this side of the Sitter.

Museums

Approaching Valère along the Schlossgasse, the visitor passes the **Majorie** (formerly housing episcopal officials), now the **Museum of Fine Arts**, and the **Archaeological Museum**. The fossil imprints of ancient Saurians found in the vicinity of Emosson are here.
Open: Tuesday to Sunday.
Valère houses the **Musée Cantonal d'Histoire et d'Ethnologie** (Museum of History and Ethnology). It offers a glimpse into history and prehistory, while what is said to be the oldest playable organ in the world (1390) is played annually during the International Festival of Old Organs.
Open: Tuesday to Sunday in summer.

Hotels and Restaurants

Recommended hotels include the **Hôtel du Rhône**, 10 rue du Scex, and **La Pergola**, 116 rue de Lausanne. Among the best places to eat are the **Enclos de Valère** and the adjacent **Caves de Tous-Vent**.

Excursion

A spectacular sight is the **Lac Souterrain** (Underground Lake of St-Léonard), a little way out of Sion on the road to Brig.

Tourist Office: place de la Planta, Sion (tel: (027) 322 8586)

◆◆ (summer)
◆◆◆ (winter)
VERBIER

Verbier, dominated by the 9,800-foot (3,000m) high Mont Gelé, is an exceptionally well-equipped resort. Haphazard building and planning do not

Curling is one of the many sports to be enjoyed at Verbier in winter

make it attractive, but still it offers superb skiing, making it one of the country's most popular winter sports resorts, especially with the younger crowd and the international community based in Geneva. There is a vast network of lifts, cable cars and ski runs, with slopes for every kind of skier, together with a good range of facilities.

Mont Gelé is reached by three cable cars; from Verbier take the cable car to Les Ruinettes, then change for Attelas I and again for Attelas II. From the cross that indicates you are at the rocky summit of Mont Gelé there are marvellous views of the Mont Blanc and Grand Combin massifs.

Hotels

There are many well-appointed hotels in the resort, the **Au Vieux-Valais** and the **Rosalp** being particularly noteworthy.

Restaurants and Entertainment

The restaurant **Gastronomique Pierroz** at the **Rosalp** is highly recommended, while the **Café La Grange** and **L'Ecurie** serve Valaisannes specialities in a charming rustic setting. For après-ski life the **Farm Club** is the most voguish venue in town.

Tourist Office: Place Centrale, CH-1936 Verbier (tel: (027) 775 3838)

◆◆◆ (summer)
◆◆◆ (winter)

ZERMATT

Surrounded by some of Europe's highest mountains –

the Dom, Matterhorn and Monte Rosa – and their great glaciers, Zermatt is one of the world's premier winter ski resorts, with near perfect skiing at an altitude which makes the snow conditions more reliable than at other resorts.

There is no motor traffic and the centre is beautifully maintained in traditional style, although cowsheds have given way to Rolex and Gucci shops and five-star hotels. It also boasts its own art gallery, the **Galerie Matterhorn**, and a museum. The **Alpine Museum** contains relics of the first conquests of the Matterhorn together with a scale model of the mountain, plus a reconstruction of 'old' Zermatt. *Open*: daily except Saturdays, Christmas to October.

Walks

Most guests visiting Zermatt in the summer come to view the Matterhorn, to walk on the mountain slopes surrounding this majestic mountain and to see the wealth of wild flowers found on the high Alpine pastures. There are short walks such as the half-hour stroll to the **Gorner** gorge with its waterfalls.

For a half-day walk you can take the **Gornergrat** rack railway, one of Europe's highest cogwheel railways, up to the Riffelberg, from where there is an excellent view of the Matterhorn, and then walk down to Zermatt via Ritti and Winkelmatten.

Skiing

In winter Zermatt is a skier's paradise, with an excellent ski area for all grades, extensive

The unmistakable outline of the Matterhorn backs the Gornergrat Railway at over 10,200 feet (3,100m)

deep-snow skiers, plus the latest artificial snow machines.

For those who prefer to take it more leisurely, there are cable cars as well as the mountain train and the underground railway up to **Sunegga**.

Hotels and Restaurants

There are 106 hotels and guest houses accommodating 18,000 guests in Zermatt. Recommended are the **Hotel Monte Rosa**, one of the oldest in town and formerly patronised by Edward Whymper – the first man to climb the Matterhorn, and enjoying panoramic views; and the luxury **Hotel Mont Cervin**, in Bahnhofstrasse, a traditional-style hotel situated in the heart of the village with a wide range of facilities. The **Romantik Hotel Julen** is a more modest traditional-style hotel.

Of the many restaurants, the **Alex Grill at the Alex Hotel** is highly recommended, while for pastries and coffee, the **Hörnli** in Bahnhofstrasse is superb.

Entertainment

The **Matterhorn-Corner** and **Matterloch** are popular bars, each with a restaurant. The lively nightspot at the **Hotel Pollux** has both disco (the **T-Bar**) and live music. Other popular discos are **Le Village** and the **Broken Ski Bar** and, for a little jazz, try the **Pink Elephant**. **Elsies Bar**, on Kirchplatz, is the most popular après-ski venue.

Tourist Office: Bahnhofplatz, CH-3920 Zermatt (tel: (027) 967 0181)

uphill transport, ample mountain restaurants, and over 100 miles (160km) of prepared pistes. Even the morning rush hour for the cable car has been alleviated by a new electric ski-bus service.

The cable car takes you up to the **Klein Matterhorn** (Little Matterhorn), the highest ski station in Europe, with spectacular views over the mountain range, and a good, easy downhill run on the glaciers. There are also black runs, gentle slopes and off-piste skiing for the experienced

WESTERN SWITZERLAND

The western part of the country contains much to interest the visitor, including Lac Léman, otherwise known as the Lake of Geneva, which has long attracted poets, artists and composers; year-round holiday resorts such as cosmopolitan Montreux and Lausanne; and the sparsely-settled region known as the Jura, where watchmaking has been a cottage industry for centuries.

◆◆ (summer)
◆◆◆ (winter)

CHATEAU D'OEX

Lying midway between the Bernese Oberland and Lac Léman, Château d'Oex (pronounced 'day') is a traditional mountain village with chalet-style houses, and a growing winter sports resort. From **La Braye**, at 5,300 feet (1,615m), there are easy and medium ski runs with four drag lifts and runs of all degrees of difficulty back down to **Pra Perron**, reached from the resort by cable car. From La Braye there is also a long run down to the hamlet of **Gerignoz**, from where a chairlift will take you up to the ski area again or a free ski-bus service will bring you back to Château d'Oex.
In both winter and summer there are numerous walking trails through pine forests and meadows. A visit to the Nature Reserve of **La Pierreuse** to see the chamois is also popular, while the most spectacular cable car ride is that from **Diablerets** village – accessible by train and postbus – to a glacier with superb views.

There is white river rafting to be had on the **River Sarine** – from May to mid-August – and canoeing, while other popular sporting pastimes include fishing for trout in the Sarine or nearby lakes such as **Rossinière** and **L'Hongrin**.
Sports facilities in the resort itself include tennis, riding, mini-golf, cycling, rock-climbing and hot-air ballooning (a famous hot-air balloon festival is held every January), and there is also a sports centre offering a sports hall, fitness room, sauna and solarium.
Although tourism is the mainstay of this valley, agriculture and craftsmanship also play an important role, reflected in the **Musée du Vieux Pays d'Enhaut** (Enhaut Traditional Museum), whose exhibits include a fine collection of engravings, paper silhouettes and stained glass windows.
Open: daily except Mondays and Wednesdays.
Also part of the museum, but located at the end of town, is the **Etambeau Chalet** (18th-century), which houses exhibitions of regional architecture.
Open: as for Musée (above).

Hotels

The **Bon-Accueil**, dating from 1756, has style; also popular is the **Alpina-Rosat**.

Entertainment

The **Richemont Bar**, with its **La Bamba**, is one of the most popular spots for dancing, while the **Le Castel** pub and the Irish Bar at the **Tavern** are also lively places. The **Keller Bar at the**

Bon-Accueil has a great ambience. In addition, there are open-air musical concerts by visiting bands and choirs, several cafés where one can relax over a glass of wine – or you could take the cable car to a mountain farm for a Swiss evening.

Tourist Office: La Place, CH-1837 Château-d'Oex (tel: (026) 924 2525)

◆◆ (summer)
◆ (winter)
FRIBOURG
Fribourg does not reveal all its delights at first glance. One must get to know the town and its soul if one is to discover its true riches. Approaching it from the east, the visitor is greeted by a surprise as he comes round a

Fribourg, clustered around its river, is an architectural treasure-trove

bend in the road, for situated on a steep bluff traced by the deep and winding course of the River Sarine ('Saane' in German), the heart of the old town unfolds in all its medieval splendour. Magnificently preserved and restored at great expense, period houses cluster about the **Cathédral Saint-Nicholas**, whose Gothic architecture contributes to the perpendicular effect of the location.

Fribourg is modest in terms of population (about 40,000), yet is impressive in terms of its protected historical buildings, its treasures of medieval religious art, its cosmopolitan population, and its importance as a centre of contemporary Christian thought.

A bilingual Catholic university, founded in 1899 and the only one in Switzerland, a renowned college, numerous institutes and seminaries, a conservatory of

music and a well-endowed library confer upon Fribourg an intellectual task of universal dimensions.

A good place to begin a visit is from the **Chapelle de Lorette**. Following the steep road descending from this vantage point, the visitor passes by the Capuchin **Convent of Montorge** and the Cistercian **Abbey of Maigrauge**. The perspective then narrows as the modern-day pilgrim enters the town itself, with its narrow, delicately curved streets and stairways, flanked by Gothic façades.

Cathedral

Heading towards the heart of the town, the way now leads upwards towards the Cathédrale Saint-Nicholas and the Bourg quarter. Witness to six centuries of history, the collegiate church, having become a cathedral when Fribourg was elevated to a bishopric, contains masterpieces in stained glass (Mehoffer 1905 and Manessier 1980) as well as a renowned organ built by Aloys Mooser and recently restored.

Museums

The **Musée d'Art et d'Histoire** (Museum of Art and History), in the elegant Renaissance Hôtel Ratzé, 227 rue Pierre-Aeby, is one of the most visited in Switzerland. In addition to numerous expositions of classical and modern art of international stature, it contains manifold collections exemplifying both local and national history and art, extending from prehistoric times to the present day. Its extension into the house known as the 'Abbatoir' (a one-time slaughterhouse) enables visitors to admire major sculptures of the Middle Ages.
Open: daily except Mondays.

The **Figurentheatermuseum** (Puppet Theatre Museum), is situated in the old town at 2 Derrière les Jardins.
Open: Saturdays and Sundays, February to December.

The **Beer Museum** in the Cardinal Brewery offers free tastings. To arrange a visit telephone: (026) 429 2211
Open: By appointment only, Monday to Friday mornings.

Hotels, Restaurants and Winebars

Recommended hotels include the **Hôtel de la Rose**, 179 place Notre Dame, and the **Hôtel Duc Berthold**, 112 rue des Bouchers.

There are over 50 restaurants: the **Buffet de la Gare** is a bustling traditional French-style brasserie. The **Marmite**, in the Duc Berthold, is one of the more exclusive venues in town.

Sports

There is an ice-skating rink, indoor swimming pool, tennis courts, horse-riding, and an 18-hole golf course seven miles away. Other activities include sculling and rowing on **Schiffenen Lake**, and even gliding, flying or short air excursions from the regional airport at **Ecuvillens**.

Tourist Office: Avenue de la Gare,1, CH-1701 Fribourg (tel: (026) 321 3175)

The Jet d'Eau forms a column of spray that gleams in the sun

◆◆◆ (summer)
◆◆◆ (winter)
GENÈVE (GENEVA) ✓

Framed by the Alps and Jura mountains, Geneva is located on the shores of the largest of the Alpine lakes: **Lac Léman** (Lake Geneva). Lakeside promenades and parks with flower beds and unexpected statues are all typical of this city, while the magnificent lake creates a leisure-resort atmosphere, an impression enhanced by the *mouettes*, or water taxis, which carry passengers from shore to shore, and by the larger boats inviting the visitor to longer lake trips. The **Jet d'Eau**, a towering spray of water over the lake, is Geneva's landmark, seen from afar during summer.

Built on both sides of the Rhône, it is a major hub of European cultural life, an important venue for international meetings, a popular centre for conventions and exhibitions, and a major financial, commercial and industrial city. Yet, thanks to its lively, cosmopolitan atmosphere, its wealth of museums, parks, excellent hotels and restaurants, it also attracts more visitors each year than any other Swiss city – and has refined the art of looking after them to a high degree.

Lower Town

The lower town, which lies between the south bank of the Rhône and the old town, is the city's main business and shopping quarter, containing rue du Rhône and other smart shopping streets such as rue de la Corraterie. In place Neuve are three of Geneva's landmarks: the **Grand-Théâtre, Conservatoire de Musique**, and the **Musée Rath** with art exhibitions (open daily).

Old Town

Don't miss the old town, with its art galleries, antique shops, book stores and typical bistros. Dominated by the **Cathédrale de Saint-Pierre** (St Peter's Cathedral) the real centre is the place du Bourg-de-Four, considered the oldest square in the city, dating back to Roman times. From an archaeological standpoint the new excavations under the cathedral are internationally important. The site dates from AD1000 and has yielded much evidence of early Christian life and art.

The cathedral was constructed in the 12th century under the Bishop de Faucigny. Built in a mixture of Romanesque and Gothic styles, it was completed in less than 60 years. The chapel to the right of the cathedral's main entrance is known as '**La Chapelle des Macchabées**' and was built in flamboyant Gothic style by the Cardinal Jean de Bogny in the 15th century.

Over the centuries the cathedral – which was called 'St Pierre' from the outset – was ravaged by fire and rebuilt on several occasions. The most important changes took place in 1756 when a portico in Graeco-Roman style was added to hide the damage caused to the face by the weather, and the cathedral's wooden steeple, which had burnt down, was replaced by the present metal one.

The **Hôtel de Ville** (town hall), not far from the cathedral in Grand-rue, is also part of Geneva's old quarter. Here you find the authorities representing the republic and the canton of Geneva. The façade of this rather austere building was begun in 1617 and finished only at the end of the 17th century, a third floor being added at the beginning of the 19th century. It contains a vast and elegant courtyard with a ramp leading up to each floor. It is the site of the founding of the International Red Cross in 1864.

Next to the town hall, on the esplanade known as La Treille, is

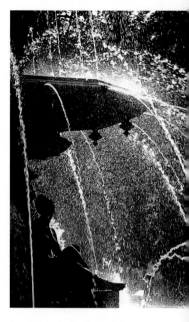

Fountain in the Jardin Anglais

a large square tower built in the latter half of the 15th century and known as the **Tour Baudet** after the former name of its locality. Opposite, on the other side of the street, is the former **arsenal** built in the first half of the 17th century for use as a granary and cereal market.

The **Maison Tavel**, which faces it on the rue du Puits-Saint-Pierre, is one of the old town's most interesting buildings. It was built in the 12th century and partially rebuilt in the 14th century.

Parks and Gardens

Geneva is rightly proud of its spacious parks with their fountains, sculptures, bandstands and cafés. Among the best are the **Jardin Anglais** on the left bank, notable for its flower clock; and the **Parc de la Grange**, with a beautiful rose garden, the site of the annual international competition of new roses.

Museums

There are 30 museums in Geneva. The **Musée d'Art et d'Histoire** (Museum of Art and History) at 2 rue Charles-Galland, houses valuable Egyptian, Greek and Roman works of art, a coin collection and an exhibition of Swiss furniture.

Open: daily.

The **Musée de l'Horlogerie** (Watch and Clock Museum), at 15 route de Malagnou, has a rare collection of 16th–20th-century

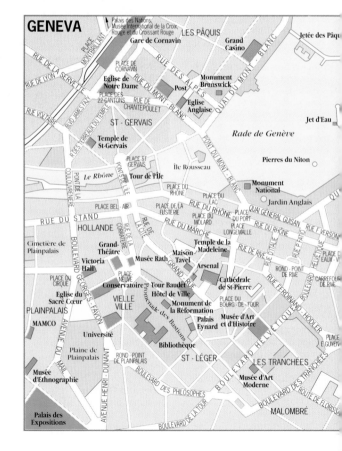

GENEVA

enamelled, decorative clocks, watches and music boxes.
Open: daily except Tuesdays.
The **Musée International de la Croix-Rouge et du Croissant-Rouge** (Museum of the Red Cross and Red Crescent), by avenue de la Paix, explores the history of the movement from its founding by Jean Henri Dunant to the present day.
Open: daily except Tuesdays.

Lac Léman (Lac de Genève)

Parc la Grange

GUSTAVE ADOR
RUE DES EAUX - VIVES
AVENUE WILLIAM-FAVRE
RUE DE MONTCHOISY
LES EAUX - VIVES
ROUTE DE FRONTENEX
AVENUE PICTET-DE-ROCHEMONT
Gare des Eaux - Vives
RUE DE LA TERRASSIÈRE
RUE DE VILLEREUSE
ROUTE DE CHÊNE
Musée d'Histoire Naturelle
ROUTE DE MALAGNOU

0   200   400 m

Accommodation
The **De La Paix**, 11 quai du Mont-Blanc, is stylish, comfortable and with an outstanding reputation, as is its near-neighbour, **Le Richemond** at jardin Brunswick. In the moderate price bracket, try the **Sagitta** at 6 rue de la Flèche, at the heart of the shopping centre. The **Beau-Rivage**, quai du Mont Blanc, is in the best tradition of Swiss hotels, closely rivalled by near-neighbours, the **Bristol**.

Entertainment
The **Grand-Théâtre** is one of the most opulent opera houses in Europe, while the **Victoria Hall** is home of the celebrated **Orchestre de la Suisse Romande**. Nightlife centres around place du Bourg-de-Four, and particularly recommended here are the bars **Mortimer**, with its famous zinc counter and **Clémence**.

Restaurants
There is an excellent fixed-price menu at **La Mère Royaume**, and the **Au Fin Bec** has a long-standing reputation for traditional Swiss dishes.

Shopping
If you have a bottomless purse you can have a field day in **Geneva**, noted for its exquisite jewellery and watches.

Excursions
Numerous excursions are possible from Geneva, thanks to its excellent location and transport facilities. One of the most popular is to the small French town of **Divonne**, located about 11 miles (18kms) away. This is noted for its

thermal baths and also for its gambling casino.

Summer visitors can also enjoy horse-racing and sailing in the resort.

Lac Léman Region

Surrounded by steep sloping vineyards, Lac Léman is the centre of sports and recreation activity for residents and visitors alike. Above the vineyards forests abound, with the Alps forming a dramatic backdrop across the lake. Steamers offer trips along the lake during the summer months. The most popular is the special tour to see the palatial homes of international film stars and business magnates which line the shores. Mont Blanc, Europe's tallest mountain, can be seen in the distance.

Thanks to the Alps which tower above it to the east and the Jura which bounds it to the west in the direction of France, the Lac Léman region has always offered outstanding opportunities for winter visitors. The Vaudois Alps, whose resorts have been constantly modernised over the years, have nevertheless remained faithful to the well-established traditions that have gained them the enviable reputation they still enjoy.

Château d'Oex, a mainly family-oriented resort (► 69), Les Mosses straddling the pass of the same name, Les Diablerets with its picturesque charm, Leysin with its youthful ambience and finally Villars with its elegant appeal, are all names that have contributed to the success of Swiss tourism.

These resorts offer countless possibilities not only to beginners and average skiers but also to those who enjoy runs requiring a high level of skill.

Cross-country skiers have not been forgotten either, and many tracks have been prepared for them through the sort of unspoilt mountain scenery dreamed of by nature lovers.

Useful Addresses

Tourist Office: 3 rue de Mont-Blanc, CH-1201 Genève (tel: (022) 909 7000)
Hospital: 24 rue Micheli-du-Crest (tel: (022) 372 3311/382 3311)

◆◆ (summer)
◆ (winter)
GRUYÈRES

The historic, medieval village, is a quaint, picturesque place with one cobblestoned street, a fountain in the centre and rows of Gothic and Renaissance houses (protected against change by a national trust), shops, restaurants and hotels. Most vehicles are banned to preserve the streets and allow a greater strolling area.

At the end of the main street is the 12th-century **Château** that housed the counts of Gruyères up to the 16th century. It is now owned by the state and is open to the public. Visitors can tour its rooms, filled with displays of period pieces. *Open*: daily.

In the castle and around the town you will notice the symbol of the counts of Gruyères – a crane (*grue* in French).

The **fromagerie** or dairy of Guyères, located at the train depot of the same name, is two hours from Geneva. Each day the local farmers collectively bring their milk to this modern facility where it is processed into Switzerland's famous Gruyère cheese. Though the plant is modernised with the latest technological machinery, the cheese itself is still made in the age-old tradition.

The step-by-step process is explained in Italian, French, German and English for the convenience of visitors. Samples of the product are offered in the café adjacent to the dairy, where visitors can also buy snacks and gifts.

Hotels

Both the **Hostellerie St-Georges** and the **Hostellerie des Chevaliers** provide comfortable accommodation in historic surroundings.

Tourist Office: CH-1663 Gruyères (tel: (025) 921 1030)

Gruyères, famous for its cheese, is a beautifully preserved medieval town

◆◆◆ (summer)
◆◆◆ (winter)
LAUSANNE ✓

Lausanne, which lies about half way along the north bank of **Lac Léman**, has a strongly individual charm, immediately arresting and inviting, but not to be enjoyed without a little effort – from Ouchy on the lakeside to the highest point of the city is a stiff climb of about 770 feet (235m). There is a convenient little railway running from the city centre (place St François) down to Ouchy, the city's port. There is a permanent holiday mood at Ouchy, where young and old throng the pavement cafés drinking wine, strolling round the boat quays or settling down to a first-class meal in one of the many restaurants. It is here, too, that the Lac Léman steamers come alongside, and where sailing boats can be hired. The successors of the inhabitants of Roman Lousonna gradually moved from the lakeside up the slopes, settling in places which could be better defended. On these ridges, where the Cité now stands, arose the **Bishop's Palace** (housing a museum with exhibits of old Lausanne) and the stately **Notre Dame Cathedral**, consecrated in 1275 by Emperor Rudolf von Habsburg and Pope Gregory X. One of the finest Gothic buildings in the country, it is one of the last places in the world to still have the tradition of the night watch. The hours from 22.00hrs until 02.00hrs are called out by a watchman looking out over the city.

At the end of the 14th century and the beginning of the 15th, the bishops built **Château St Maire**, which is now used as the seat of the canton government. Around this nucleus grew the modern city. Today, bridges link the various parts of Lausanne: Grand Pont, Pont-Bessières and Pont-Chaudro. Above and below the bridges are houses which often cling so closely to the hillsides that they have entrances on several levels.

Museums
The **Palais de Rumine** (Rumine Palace), built at the beginning of this century, houses Lausanne University and several museums covering fine arts, history, natural history and botany.
Open: Tuesday to Sunday.
The **Musée Olympique** (Olympic Museum) at 18 avenue Ruchonnet, traces the history of the Olympic Games.
Open: daily in summer; daily except Mondays in winter.

Festivals and Fairs
The headquarters of the Federal Court, the International Committee for the Olympic Games and the many international fairs and congresses have given Lausanne an international reputation. Many of the exhibitions and other events take place in the **Palais de Beaulieu** where there is also one of the biggest and most modern of Switzerland's theatres. And it is here that every year from May to July for the past 24 years, well-known artists of the world of music and dance have gathered together. Lausanne puts on its happiest

and most hospitable face during the last week of June for the city festival.

Flower-seller in Lausanne. The town is a lively and cultured centre for French-speaking Switzerland

Hotels and Restaurants
There are several really excellent hotels in Lausanne, the **Beau-Rivage Palace** being probably the best of all, set in a large park on the shores of the lake in Ouchy.
The **Girardet** in the **Hotel de Ville** is so renowned that diners are asked to book months in advance for dinner. Also good are **La Grappe d'Or** at 3 rue Cheneau-de-Bourg, The **Café Beau-Rivage** in the hotel of the same name, and **La Voile d'Or** in Vidy. For delicious

pastries, you should try the **Café Manuel** in place St François.

Shopping
Many first-class stores are found along the rue St François and the rue du Bourg. Good buys are watches and jewellery, leather goods and chocolates.

Excursions
There is a fascinating military museum in the nearby small town of **Morges**, containing

79

weapons and uniforms dating from the early 16th century, as well as the Museum Alexis Forel with an important collection of dolls, toys and games.

Open: daily except Mondays.

Nyon is a popular summer resort flanking the lake, with a 13th-century castle currently closed for restoration.

Tourist Office: 2 avenue Rhodanie, CH-1007 Lausanne (tel: (021) 613 7373)

◆◆ (summer)
◆◆◆ (winter)
LES DIABLERETS

The holiday resort of Les Diablerets is situated some 3,900 feet (1,200m) above sea-level in the very heart of the Vaudois Alps at the foot of a mountain range capped by a breathtaking glacier. Parallel development of agriculture and tourism is one of the characteristics of this mountain village which dates from the Middle Ages, and which today offers the visitor a wide choice of accommodation in hotels, rented apartments and chalets.

In summer Les Diablerets is the starting point for many walks or hikes across an extensive nature reserve, with a wide network of marked paths. An excursion to the **Diablerets glacier** is a very special experience. It takes an aerial cable car only 35 minutes to reach the glacier at 9,800 feet (3,000m) above sea-level, where the snow never melts and where visitors can often enjoy summer skiing or set off for walks and mountain tours. There are also guided trips on a snow-bus across the glacier. To complete its wide range of activities, Les Diablerets can also offer sports such as mountain climbing, tennis, swimming, fishing in mountain streams and lakes, rafting, riding, miniature golf,

The mountains around Les Diablerets are a paradise for keen walkers

and an 18-hole golf course near by.

Hotels

Les Diablerets is one of the best hotels in Les Diablerets, with an attractive dining room that enjoys a high reputation for the standard of its cuisine. **Hôtel Les Diablotins** offers less expensive accommodation in a mountain setting.

Tourist Office: Case postale 42, Bâtiment BCV, CH-1856 Les Diablerets (tel: 025 531358)

◆◆ (summer)
◆◆◆ (winter)
LEYSIN

Located in the Vaudois Alps, Leysin is one of the most delightful mountain resorts in Switzerland, known for its refreshing, invigorating and sunny climate, its attractive surroundings and its superb Alpine panoramas.

The history of this international health resort dates back to 1890 when the sleepy mountain village was discovered by famous doctors and became known worldwide as a centre for treating lung and bone diseases. Huge sanatoria and hotels were built, but after World War II the sanatoria gradually emptied.

In the 1950s the focus in Leysin shifted from being a mountain health resort to becoming a leisure resort. Today, those seeking rest and relaxation, nature-lovers or those interested in active sports, can choose from a wide range of activities and facilities in both summer and winter.

For summer visitors there is an extensive network of marked paths throughout the whole region: climbing courses are offered by the Leysin mountaineering school; and there are gondola lifts to take visitors to the **Mayen Alp** or to the **Berneuse** peak where they can enjoy a magnificent view from the Bernese Alps to the Mont-Blanc massif. Coach excursions to the Diablerets glacier, Montreux or Geneva are readily available.

There are indoor or open air facilities and centres for such sports as tennis, table tennis, squash, indoor golf, miniature golf, swimming, fishing, riding, hang-gliding and skating. And at **Aigle**, some 20 minutes away, there is an 18-hole golf course. In winter, Leysin offers excellent skiing for beginners and intermediates. There are two main cable cars, La Berneuse and Mayen, plus numerous ski or chairlifts and several nursery slopes.

Hotels and Restaurants

Among the best hotels are the **Hôtel Central-Residence**, **Le Relais-Regency** and the **Mont-Riant**. The restaurant **Le Leysin** specialises in dishes *au feu de bois* (cooked in a wood-fire oven).

Entertainment

Leysin is more suited to families and those who are happy with quiet evenings rather than to swinging visitors who like to dance the night away.

Tourist Office: CH-1854 Leysin (tel: (024) 494 2244)

Montreux, on the shore of Lac Léman, is a romantic sight at nightfall

◆◆◆ (summer)
◆◆◆ (winter)
MONTREUX ✓

Since the 18th-century writer Jean-Jacques Rousseau chose the Montreux area as the setting for his novel *La Nouvelle Héloise*, the town has developed into one of the most popular and populated places on **Lac Léman**. Its geographical position is superb, being on a wide bay, open to the south, with wooded hills and sloping vineyards to the rear protecting the whole area from north and east winds. The lake stores the heat, reflects the light, and makes Montreux's climate delightful.

It is the mildest area north of the Alps with an average annual temperature of 10°C (50°F), to which the extraordinary vegetation bears witness. There is a wealth of trees and plants, some of them subtropical, on the *quais* – a paradise for strollers – between Clarens and Chillon Castle. Fig and almond trees flourish, as do laurels and eucalyptus; there are cypresses, magnolias and palm trees, and every spring the whole town resembles a huge bouquet, with its higher-lying pastures covered with thousands of narcissi.

Present-day Montreux developed out of 20 former hamlets. Apart from its wide modern streets there is also an old quarter with picturesque alleys located higher up the slopes. And those who venture still higher can enjoy an enchanting panorama from Glion, Caux, Les Avants or Sonloup.

Lake and mountains – and the carefully tended parks in the town, where one can sit and enjoy the view – are an invitation to rest. Although Montreux retains a handful of luxury hotels belonging to a past era, many modern hotels and buildings show that the town is not prepared to rest on its laurels. And thanks to its wide range of hotels, offering a total of 4,000 beds, its conference and exhibition centre and its casino, Montreux is increasingly becoming a meeting place for people from all four corners of the globe.

Château de Chillon (Chillon Castle)

One of Montreux's chief attractions, and one of the best preserved medieval castles in Europe, is the beautiful 13th-century Chillon Castle. Immortalised by Lord Byron in his poem *The Prisoner of Chillon*, this one-time prison stands on a rock promontory jutting into the lake, south of the town. *Open*: daily.

Festivals

In spring there is the Golden Rose (Rose d'Or) international television competition and rock festival; in July, the Jazz Festival; in September, the Classical Music Festival, to mention but a few local events. Popular local festivals and other cultural activities help to ensure that there is always something going on for visitors to enjoy.

Hotels

Of the luxury hotels the **Montreux Palace**, 100 Grand-rue, and **Grand Hotel Excelsior**, 21 rue Bon Port, are world famous, and the first class **Suisse et Majestic**, 43 avenue des Alpes, with its traditionally styled bedrooms, some overlooking the lake, can also be recommended. Of the moderately priced hotels the **Helvétie**, 32 avenue du Casino, is extremely good, with a pleasant roof terrace.

Restaurants

The **Restaurant Francais**, of the **Suisse et Majestic** hotel, with its attractive furnishings and excellent cuisine is popular. Any of the three restaurants in the classy **Hotel Eden au Lac** are also recommended.

Excursions

There are mountain railways to transport the visitor into a wonderland of sights and experiences; on **Rochers-de-Naye**, 6,700 feet (2,042m) above sea-level, the restaurant **Plein Roc** built into the rock face offers a stunning view; and the Montreux-Bernese Oberland Railway offers excursions to such places as **Château D'Oex** and **Gstaad** (➤ 69 and 37).

Tourist Office: 5 avenue du Théâtre, CH-1820 Montreux (tel: (021) 962 8484)

◆◆ (summer)
◆ (winter)

NEUCHÂTEL

Neuchâtel, a charming town located on the edge of its lake (Lake Neuchâtel) and at the foot of Chaumont, has much to interest the visitor, including the 12th-century Collegiate Church, the castle (mainly 15th- and 16th-century), and the old part of town with its ancient fountains and patrician houses. In addition it has museums (see below), an excellent library and an active cultural life thanks to its being a university town.

The countryside and lakeshore bordering Neuchâtel provide ample scope for relaxation and walking. Here you will find picturesque villages and old fortified towns such as **Grandson**, vineyards, fields and woods, beaches, swimming pools, castles and museums, as well as facilities for nautical sports, fishing and camping. **Yverdon-les-Bains**, a well-known spa resort, offers what is said to be the biggest outdoor thermal pool in Switzerland.

Museums
The **Musée d'Art et d'Histoire** (Art and History Museum) contains a large collection of French Impressionist works, plus a world-famous collection of music boxes and automated dolls. A demonstration of the music boxes takes place the first Sunday in each month.
Open: daily except Mondays.
The **Musée Cantonal d'Archéologie** (Archaeological Museum) has many exhibits found in local caves dating back 50,000 years.
Open: Tuesday to Sunday, afternoons only.

Hotels and Restaurants
The **Beaulac**, overlooking the lake is the best in town. The **Marché** is central and excellent value. Of the numerous restaurants, **La Maison des Halles**, a brasserie that serves seasonal specialities and cooks pizzas in a wood-fired oven, is always a good bet. For mouth-watering pastries there is **Wodey-Suchard**.

Excursions
There are popular excursions to **Chaumont** and to the **Jura heights**, or you can cruise on the three Jurassian lakes. **St Ursanne** on the River Doubs, **Porrentruy** in the Ajoie, and **Delémont** with its prince-bishop's castle, all have architectural treasures.

Tourist Office: Hotel des Postes, CH-2001 Neuchâtel (tel:(032) 889 6890)

◆◆ (summer)
◆◆ (winter)
VEVEY
Vevey, on Lac Léman, is a 'Swiss Riviera' resort with an interesting history, having been at the

Charlie Chaplin in Vevey; the town hosts a comedy film festival

crossroads of Europe since the Roman Empire. It prospered as trade expanded in the Middle Ages and further progressed on the arrival of the French Huguenots. Tourists began discovering its attractions in the 19th century.

The lakeside promenade, which extends for more than 5½ miles (9km), is noted for its lovingly tended flower beds. And Lac Léman also provides Vevey visitors with a wide range of watersports and cruising opportunities.

Every Monday and Saturday the Vevey marketplace comes alive with an exhilarating open market, which often includes local wine tastings. Roughly four times a century (last in 1999), Vevey celebrates a 'Winegrowers' Festival' (*Fête des Vignerons*) which includes a huge wine pageant with thousands of people participating.

The resort is also a mecca for musicians and film-makers; it is the venue for the Clara Haskil piano competition and the International Comedy Film Festival; and, together with Montreux, is host to the annual Montreux-Vevey Music Festival.

Museums

Together with wine and tourism, chocolate is Vevey's other mainstay. The famous Nestlé corporation has its headquarters here and the **Alimentarium** (Museum of Nutrition) at 1 rue du Léman was founded by the company. It covers the natural science, ethnography and history of food.
Open: daily except Mondays,

April to October.
Also of interest is the **Musée Suisse d'Appareils Photographiques** (Swiss Museum of Cameras) at 4 Grande Place, a collection of cameras from the late 19th century to the present.
Open: daily except Mondays, April to October.

Mont Pèlerin

A 10-minute ride by funicular or car up to Mont-Pèlerin, a region of woods, farms and villas, is highly recommended. The view from here is considered by many to be one of the best in Switzerland, taking in Lac Léman, Vevey, Montreux, the Rhône Valley and the French Alps. You can, if you wish, return to the lakeside on foot, visiting the picturesque medieval village of **Chardonne** on the way.

Hotels and Restaurants

The leading hotel of Vevey is the **Trois Couronnes**, 49 rue d'Italie, beautifully situated overlooking the lake and which was the setting for the film *Daisy Miller*. Among the best restaurants are **Du Raisin**, and **Restaurant du Rivage** with its idyllic lakeside terrace.

Excursions

Vevey is a good starting point for excursions. The range is wide: a leisurely drive among the vineyards; a variety of short or long boat trips on the lake; a cogwheel train ride to soak up the glorious mountain scenery along the way to **Gstaad**; or panoramic views from **Les Pléiades** or **Rochers-de-Naye**.

Tourist Office: Grand Place 29 Gare, CH-1800 Vevey (tel: (021) 922 2020)

◆◆ (summer)
◆◆◆ (winter)
VILLARS

At 4,265 feet (1,300m) above sea-level on a plateau high above the Rhône valley, and commanding a superb panoramic view of the Vaudois Alps, the Valaisan Alps, and Mont Blanc, Villars is one of Switzerland's premier winter resorts – and one of the best equipped.

In summer too there is plenty to do. For walkers there are 186 miles (300km) of marked paths, and excursions are organised on which the visitor can enjoy a view of the whole Alpine chain, for example by taking an aerial cable car to the **Roc d'Orsay** at 6,500 feet

Summer visitors to Villars can enjoy the outdoor swimming pool

(2,000m). In Villars itself the New Sporting leisure club offers squash and tennis courts, volley ball, badminton, a Turkish bath and an amazing, electronically controlled 18-hole golf course simulator. Other resort facilities include indoor and outdoor swimming pools, an ice-skating rink, miniature golf, and a real 18-hole golf course.

There are also facilities for bowling, parachuting and fishing in mountain lakes as well as a fitness club and circuit. Tennis and golf tournaments are held in summer, as are table-tennis and petanque competitions.

In winter the resort offers 75 miles (120km) of prepared pistes, ranging from gentle nursery slopes to the 9,800-foot (3,000m) high glacier at **Les Diablerets** (▶ 80), linked to the Villars ski region.

Other winter activities include cross-country skiing, ice-skating and delightful mountain walks along the many well-marked footpaths.

The ancient spa town of **Bex** (pronounced 'Bey'), a short drive down the valley, is well worth a visit.

Hotels

The four-star **Panorama Hotel** is well run and nicely furnished, with facilities that include a heated swimming pool, sauna, solarium, lounge, spacious bar and sun terrace.

The **Hôtel du Golf et Marie-Louise**, situated in the village centre, is a charming family-run hotel furnished in traditional Swiss style.

The royal residence of Vaduz Castle

Entertainment

There are several discos such as **El Gringo** and **The Fox**. **Charlie's Bar** has regular theme nights, at least one of which is bound to appeal to younger visitors, while **Bar le Coq Hardi** at the Grand Hotel du Parc is a piano bar better suited to those seeking a quiet night.

Tourist Office: CH-1884 Villars-sur-Ollon (tel: (024) 495 3232)

LIECHTENSTEIN

With Switzerland to its west and south and Austria to its east lies Liechtenstein, tiny, independent and extremely prosperous. Liechtenstein has been around since 1719, when the domain of Schellenberg and the county of Vaduz were welded into an independent principality – a little gem of a country just over 15 miles (25km) long and 3¾ miles (6km) wide. With not quite 30,000 inhabitants occupying a total area of 62 square miles (160sq km), it is a microscopic geographical unit; yet despite being so tiny it is divided politically into an upper region – once the county of **Vaduz** – and a lower region, formerly the domain of **Schellenberg**. It comprises a total of 11 autonomous communities which together offer an extensive range of attractions – museums, boutiques, hotels, restaurants, historical sites, vineyards and plenty of sports facilities – but at the same time retains its own very individual charm and appeal.

Liechtenstein is also a family-oriented place, with adventure playgrounds to keep children happy. There are exhibitions, amateur theatre productions, folklore and intellectually stimulating concerts, while the **Theater am Kirchplatz** in

Schaan presents entertainment of every kind – films, ballet, pop singers, plays and children's theatre, clowns and dramatised fairy tales.

◆◆ (summer)
◆ (winter)

VADUZ

As one might expect, the biggest community, Vaduz, is the capital and also the main tourist centre. Located close to the right shore of the Rhein at the foot of the mighty Rätikon peak, it was once a village primarily known for its excellent wine, but has developed into a busy capital with industry, banks, offices and service industries. It is dominated by Vaduz castle, the prince's residence built around 1300. The castle is not open to the public.

Art Collection

A main attraction for visitors is the Art Gallery housed in the Englanderbau at Städtle 37. The works are chiefly from the collection of the Princes of Liechtenstein – one of the oldest and most comprehensive private collections in Europe. Peter Paul Rubens' subtle portraits of his children by his first marriage are exhibited, as well as his monumental cycle of paintings of the Roman Consul, Decius Mus.
Open: daily.

Postmuseum

Liechtenstein's postage stamps, tiny works of art featuring scenes of the countryside and reproductions of paintings in the royal art collection, are highly regarded by philatelists throughout the world. The Postage Stamp Museum, Städtle 37, has a large collection of the most distinctive Liechtenstein stamps dating back to 1912. Entrance free.
Open: daily.

Mountain Walks

Depending on mood and physical condition, you can stroll alongside a swirling mountain brook with the family, grill sausages over an open fire and, after a snooze, help the children build a dam across the brook; or you can follow reliably marked footpaths through the romantic valleys, up across sun-drenched terraces into the seclusion of the Alps. The famous **Furstensteig**, a marked footpath starting from Gaflei, offers marvellous views over the Rhine Valley. The little resort of Malbun also provides excellent mountain walks.

Formalities

There are no customs formalities on the Liechtenstein-Swiss border. Such formalities do exist, however, on the border to Austria's federal state of Vorarlberg north of Liechtenstein. Entry and customs regulations are the same as for Switzerland.

Hotels and Restaurants

Vaduz offers 340 beds in nine hotels and inns, mainly small establishments. The youth hostel Schaan/Vaduz, with 80 beds, is located between Vaduz and Schaan.

Liechtenstein National Tourist Office, Städtle 37, PO Box 139, FL-9490 Vaduz (tel: (075) 232 1443 or 392 1111)

PEACE AND QUIET

Wildlife and Countryside in Switzerland
by Paul Sterry

The visitor to Switzerland is confronted with natural beauty at every turn. From the imposing, snow-covered peaks of the Eiger or the Jungfrau to immense glaciers eroding Alpine valleys and the dazzling array of colour to be found in the flower-rich meadows, there is always something of interest. Scenic beauty is not confined to the uplands of the Alps and the Jura, however; the low-lying land between the mountain ranges, studded with tranquil lakes and lush pastures, provides a peaceful contrast. The distribution of Switzerland's wildlife is strongly linked to altitude, some species preferring lowland areas and others found only on the highest peaks. Being able to recognise elevation by the vegetation, therefore, will help the visitor to know what species to look for.

Towns, Parks and Gardens
Without venturing far you can often enjoy a surprising variety of wildlife, and in particular several species of birds. If staying in the mountains, alpine species may be seen, especially during the winter when they descend to the lower slopes, while at lower altitudes, the species tend to be those otherwise found on the edges of woodland.

In western Europe, hawfinches are generally secretive woodland birds, but in Switzerland, as in many other countries further east, they seem to cohabit with man quite successfully and are often seen in parks and gardens with mature trees. The reverse is the case with the robin, however,

Swifts
One of the most familiar summer sounds in small Swiss towns is that of screaming swifts. Parties of these aerobatic birds skim through the streets at breakneck speed uttering their shrill call. Nests are built under eaves and in the roofs of houses, and this species seldom breeds away from human dwellings.

which is a familiar garden bird in some countries, but in Switzerland is a shy bird found only in natural woodland. In Swiss gardens, its place is taken by another superficially similar bird, the black redstart. Also found among boulders and scree on mountainsides, this charming little bird often nests in outhouses and old walls.

Lowland Valleys and Agricultural Land
A considerable part of Switzerland is comparatively low-lying, being under 3,000 feet (900m) above sea level. The Mittelland runs from the Bodensee (Lake Constance) in the east to Lac Léman (Lake Geneva) in the west. Many of the rolling hills and valleys have been given over to agriculture and this charming region also contains much of the country's human population.

Flower-rich grazing meadows are a colourful sight, with a wealth of flowers of many species. Grasshoppers and crickets scurry among the vegetation and many fall victim

Goldfinches feed on seed heads

to the hovering kestrels or great grey shrikes, which use fence posts and overhead wires as vantage points. These same perches are often used by corn buntings, whose buzzing song, which is supposed to resemble jangling keys, is a familiar sound of the Swiss lowlands. Sunny south-facing slopes, particularly around the shores of Lac Léman, often have vineyards which are the haunt of red-backed shrikes and ortolan buntings. The former often sit on prominent perches, ever alert for passing insects, while the latter are more secretive and creep along furrows in the ground.

Lakes, Rivers and Freshwater

Wherever a river feeds or drains one of the large, natural lakes, a small delta often forms. Exposed shingle ridges sometimes have breeding little ringed plovers, and water plants, reedbeds and wet woodland add to the diversity. The sanctuary that this provides is a haven for breeding birds such as coots, mallards, little grebes and water rails as well as many less numerous species. Great crested grebes also nest here, and in early spring pairs can be seen performing their elaborate courtship displays on the open water, each partner holding water plants in its beak. Springtime sees the arrival of many migrant birds from south of the Mediterranean which come to breed in the tangled waterside vegetation. Reed, great reed and Savi's warblers sometimes sing from exposed perches and find the abundant supply of insects such as midges, caddis flies and mayflies richly repays their journey north. The waters of many of the lakes have large populations of fish and amphibians, which in turn feed many species of bird: little bitterns and grey herons silently stalk the shallows and black kites scavenge any remains they leave.

Deciduous Forest

Thanks to strict Swiss forestry laws, the foothills of the Alps and the Jura are still, in part, cloaked in woodland. Here the trees are mostly deciduous, especially beech, occasionally interspersed with conifers, and hold a wide range of woodland wildlife. Pure stands of beech support only a limited range of plants and animals when compared to more mixed woodlands. The leaf canopy is so dense that only the most shade-tolerant plants can grow on the woodland floor. However, in spring beech woodlands come alive with the song of wood warblers, often accompanied by chiffchaffs and Bonelli's warblers in clearings and rides. Great spotted and black woodpeckers are most easily seen here in spring. Where a variety of tree species occurs, marsh tits, firecrests and even golden orioles may be found. The latter's fluty song is evocative of the tropics and carries far on a still morning. Around farms the woodland has often been cleared to create grazing pastures. This effectively increases the woodland edge, which often allows better views of wildlife than the woodland interior, and the patchwork landscape is particularly favoured by grey-headed woodpeckers and pied flycatchers, while roe deer may occasionally venture into the open to graze.

Upland Forests

As the appearance of the forest changes, the wildlife it contains also changes. Although birds such as black woodpecker and great spotted woodpecker appear to thrive in almost any forest of reasonable size in Switzerland, the increase in altitude brings with it an interesting addition – the three-toed woodpecker, recognisable by its black-and-white striped face. Nutcrackers are common and are often seen perched on the tops of trees, while in the lower branches, redpolls, crested tits and willow tits all forage for insects. Nearer the tree line the

birdwatcher will begin to encounter citril finches. These delightful little yellow-green birds build neat nests among the branches of the conifers and sometimes descend to lower altitudes outside the breeding season. Europe's largest gamebird, the capercaillie, is sometimes disturbed by ramblers from among piles of fallen branches. Its smaller relative, the hazelhen, although quiet and unobtrusive, is rather less timid and if spotted will sometimes sit motionless, staring back at the observer.

Above the Tree Line

Above an altitude of about 6,000 feet (1,800m) the trees become stunted and gradually disappear to be replaced by areas of low scrub and scree and boulder fields. At the highest elevations, glaciers and permanent snow fields dominate the landscape, but right up to their edge, creeping and low-growing vegetation, such as mosses, dwarf willows, saxifrages and sandworts, persists. Where the soil is sufficiently loose, alpine marmots dig their burrows and form loose colonies and, among the boulders, rock thrushes, rock partridges and ptarmigan feed and make their nests.

Rocky outcrops are also the haunt of chamois, sure-footedly crossing gulleys and rock faces. The most magnificent creature of all, however, is the ibex. Small colonies of these wild goats, such as that at Piz Albris, still survive.

The skies high above the peaks are the domain of golden eagles and peregrine falcons, and the occasional griffon vulture drifts by, ever alert for casualties of this inhospitable terrain. Ravens sometimes mob these birds of prey if they pass too close to the raven's territory. Their relative, the alpine chough, is much more numerous. Like other crows, they are quick to learn and will accost human visitors for food.

Alpine Meadows

These meadows, grazed by cattle during the summer months, are a riot of colour from May until August. Daisies, knapweeds, bellflowers and hay-rattles grow in profusion, and, in wet hollows, clumps of butterworts, louseworts and marsh marigold add to the variety. Here and there among the commoner species, those with a keen eye may spot the orchids which also thrive in these pastures. Burnt orchids and the creamy-white spikes of the elder-flowered orchids are widespread, favouring meadows where the underlying soil is limestone.

Alpine meadows often echo with the sound of a loud, whistling call, the source of which is not a bird but a mammal, and a very curious one at that. Alpine marmots are large rodents with course fur which live in burrows among tussocks of grass. Although they often become indifferent to the presence of man, they remain ever alert for predators such as the golden eagle and the shrill alarm call serves to alert fellow marmots.

Specialised Alpine Flowers

Above the tree line, the scree slopes and boulder fields are the highest habitats to support plant life before the domain of permanent snow and ice is reached. These peaks are among the most inhospitable places on earth, yet, despite the rigours of the environment, spring and summer bring about a transformation in the landscape with alpine plants bursting into an array of colour. With the snows often not thawing until April or May and reappearing again often as early as September, plants have a short growing season in which to flower and produce seeds and build up stores for the coming winter. Many do not even wait until the snow has cleared completely and the charming, nodding flowers of the alpine snowbell push their way through the melting snow. These are followed shortly after by hardy crocuses and several species of gentians, the most attractive of which is perhaps the spring gentian, whose blue flowers stud the vegetation. White flowers of sandworts and pearlworts seem to grow out of bare rock and a careful search of short turf may even reveal the diminutive grass-like false musk orchid. The flowers that grow in the true alpine zone (*ie* above the tree line) are extremely specialised; many are dwarfed or creeping, thus avoiding the fierce, biting winds, and are rather slow-growing, but some are more showy. The alpenrose, which, despite its name, is a dwarf species of *Rhododendron*, is one of the most attractive, its rose-coloured flowers adorning the low-growing bushes, but its less showy companion, edelweiss, is the best-known alpine species.

Winter Wildlife

Although many animals either hibernate or migrate to escape the winter, some remain active throughout the year. When weather conditions are particularly harsh, some are lured close to human habitation. Snow finches and alpine accentors search inconspicuously for seeds and hibernating insects among rocks and vegetation and often feed close to skilifts. The disturbance caused by the human visitors does not seem to upset them unduly. Chamois haunt rocky outcrops and stand out conspicuously if seen against a blanket of snow. Ptarmigan, on the other hand, have plumage which varies according to the season and blend in with their natural surroundings. The white winter feathers match the snow and help the bird avoid detection by golden eagles. This seasonal change in appearance is not confined to the bird world and 'ermine' stoats are often seen by skiers.

Many of the country's larger lakes, such as Lakes Constance and Neuchâtel, are important wintering sites for waterbirds, mainly because they almost invariably remain ice-free. Lac Léman, which is the largest lake in western Europe, is one of the most important of such sites and estimates of between 50,000 and 100,000 coots, gulls and ducks (in particular tufted duck and pochard) are usual.

Spring gentians in an Alpine meadow

93

FOOD AND DRINK

Switzerland has no lack of good restaurants offering a wide choice of specialities. There is not really any such thing as Swiss cuisine, only regional foods and dishes which are nourishing, wholesome and often country-style. Specialities include Neuchâtel tripe; *Berner Platte*, a Bernese dish of boiled meat and sausages served with haricot beans; *rösti*, grated fried potatoes; St Gallen sausages (*Bratwurst*); *papet* from the canton of Vaud (leeks with potatoes); Ticinese *risotto*; Basel's brown-flour soup (*Mehlsuppe*) and onion flans; Zürich's shredded veal (*schnitzeltes Kalbfleisch*); barley soup and air-dried meats (*Bundnerfleisch*) from the Grisons; and of course all the cheeses – Gruyère (*Greyerze* in German and Groviera in Italian), Emmentaler, Appenzeller, Jura, the French-Swiss *tommes*, and the herb cheeses from Eastern Switzerland, plus the famous cheese dishes *fondue*, *raclette* and cheese flans.

Nor should the visitor overlook the many fish dishes, the endless varieties of bread, the red and white wine specially chosen to go with each of these dishes, the range of spirits, Kirsch, Williamine, marc and grappa, and finally the ciders and mineral waters.

Then there are the cakes and confectionery: *cuchaules* and *taillaules* (breads eaten on Sundays), butter cakes and *bricelets* from the

A typical hearty meal in one of the many waterfront restaurants which combine eating with a view

French-speaking part of
Switzerland, Kirsch gâteau from
Zug, Unterwalden's scrambled
pancakes, pear bread from
central Switzerland, carrot
gâteau from Aargau, *Leckerli*
honey biscuits from Basel,
Bernese meringues, and nut
cake from the Grisons.

Menus
It is important to note that the
'menu' is *Karte* in German-
speaking Switzerland and *carte*
in the French-speaking part. If
you ask for a 'menu' the waiter
is more likely to return with the
dish of the day, since that is what
the word means to the Swiss.
All *Karten* have a *menu*, which is
usually the chef's special at a
moderate price; this may also
be listed as *Tagesplatte*,
Tagesteller or *plat du jour*,
depending on whether the
language is German or French.

Wines and Spirits
Switzerland has eight wine
areas and as many vintners as
there are sunny slopes for
growing grapes. The major
areas are Geneva (red and
white wines), Neuchâtel and
Vaud (white), the southern
Valais (white Fendant and red
Dôle), the Ticino (red Merlot),
and Graubünden (red Veltliner).
Fruit brandies are a popular
Swiss speciality.

Swiss Chocolates
As well as the famous names of
Tobler, Nestlé and Lindt &
Sprüngli, look out for the
products of gourmet
chocolatiers such as Moreau,
found in the Neuchâtel region,
and Zürich-based Teuscher.

SHOPPING
Switzerland's superb products
make it a shopper's paradise.
Fine watches come in an infinite
variety. More good buys are
textiles, embroideries, fine
handkerchiefs, woollen
sportswear and linen.
Chocolates come in an amazing
variety of sizes, shapes and
flavours. Other good buys
include precision instruments,
drafting sets, multi-blade pocket
knives, music boxes,
woodcarvings, ceramics and
other handmade items, antiques
and art books.
Generally shops are open from
08.00/09.00hrs until 18.30hrs
from Monday to Friday and
08.00/ 09.00hrs until 16.00/
17.00hrs on Saturday. In large
towns some shops may close
Monday mornings, while in
suburban areas and small towns,
shops normally close on
Wednesday or Thursday
afternoon. In some areas shops
may close for lunch.

ACCOMMODATION
Hotels
Swiss hotels are the envy of
hoteliers throughout the world,
and understandably so in view
of their exceptionally high
standards, both in terms of
accommodation and service.
The Swiss Hotel Association
(SHA, Schweizer Hotelier-
Verein, Monbijoustrasse 130,
CH-3001, Bern, tel: (031)
507111) publishes a yearly
guide of 2,680 hotels and
pensions which are members.
The guide shows the rates,
addresses, telephone/telex
numbers, opening dates and

amenities of the various hotels. The SHA also publishes a list of hotels that offer special terms for senior citizens, mostly between the main holiday seasons. In addition, the *Swiss Hotel Guide for the Disabled* contains details about hotels for guests confined to a wheelchair (see **Disabled Travellers** and **Senior Citizens** sections in the **Directory***).* These guides are all available from the Swiss National Tourist Office. A list of hotels and restaurants catering for Jewish visitors can also be obtained from the SNTO.

The SNTO does not make hotel reservations, however. Visitors are therefore advised to book direct with the hotel or through a travel agent or hotel representative. Those wishing to make advance reservations may obtain advice on arrival at local tourist offices, during business hours. Some main railway stations and airports have hotel reservation facilities.

Chalets and Apartments

Information regarding the rental of chalets, houses and furnished apartments for holidays is available from local tourist offices and estate agents in Switzerland. A list of contacts is available from the SNTO.

Youth Hostels

Youth hostel accommodation is available to visitors up to the age

Despite its grand size, the Palace Hotel in Gstaad prides itself on being a traditional 'family pension'

of 25 years. Hostellers over 25 are admitted if there is room. Visitors from abroad must hold a membership card of their national organisation affiliated to the International Youth Hostels Federation. To avoid disappointment, wardens of youth hostels should be given prior notice (at least five days) of arrival. The SNTO publishes a list of Swiss Youth Hostels. The local association is: Schweizerischer Bund für Jungendherbergen (Swiss Youth Hostel Association), Neufeldstrasse 9, CH-3012 Bern 22 (tel: (031) 245503).

CULTURE, ENTERTAINMENT, NIGHTLIFE

Entertainment

Entertainment opportunities in Switzerland are boundless. Whatever the season the visitor will encounter festivals, folklore performances, concerts and the like both during the day and evening. In all the principal ski resorts there is always something happening after the day's sport, including lively discothèques and night-clubs which continue into the small hours. The same applies to the major cities and towns, even though the Swiss are not by nature night owls – hardly surprising since most of them start work at 07.00hrs! However, the early start certainly does not deter them from joining in the fun of the many carnivals staged throughout the country, such as that in Basel in February, or in the lively celebrations marking Swiss National Day on 1 August.

All can join in the fun of carnival, and plenty such events take place, particularly at Mardi Gras

Generally speaking, the concert and theatre season runs from September to May, but in summer, music festivals are organised by several Swiss cities – the most prestigious of which is the one held in Luzern. Jazz lovers will not be disappointed either, especially if they are in Montreux in the summer for the annual festival. Lists of events including art exhibitions, music festivals, folklore programmes and sporting events are obtainable from SNTO.

Gambling

Gambling in Switzerland is restricted to boule, and the maximum stake that can be placed is Sfr 5.

97

HOW TO BE A LOCAL

Correctness and reliability are key Swiss characteristics. Buses run on time – to the second; laws are diligently observed; and fairness and quality are highly valued. Switzerland is not a showy place, and the Swiss reserve can give an initial impression of coldness. But you will find that, behind this restraint, there lies a diverse and welcoming society. Since the Swiss enjoy one of the highest standards of living in the world, experiencing Switzerland as the locals do inevitably implies having a healthy sufficiency of funds at your disposal. But even those Swiss on limited budgets can make the most of the good things this country offers: by avoiding, for instance, except on very special occasions, the restaurants, cafés and bars enjoying the best locations, and patronising instead the smaller establishments found away from the main tourist haunts; by opting for the excellent public transport rather than expensive taxis; and by enjoying the various – free – carnivals, street processions and folklore events.

PERSONAL PRIORITIES

Female visitors to Switzerland – including those travelling independently – should encounter few problems. In some of the remoter mountain villages and the staunchly Roman Catholic Ticino region, single women on their own are sometimes regarded with slight suspicion, but generally speaking Switzerland is a safe and welcoming country for all visitors. Unwanted sexual advances by locals, for instance, are extremely rare: it is fellow visitors that the female traveller should be on her guard against. Hardly surprisingly, in view of its huge pharmaceutical industry, all leading legal drugs are available in Switzerlands' pharmacies. Not all are readily available over the counter and, as in the UK, pharmacists will require a prescription from a Swiss-registered medical practitioner.

CHILDREN

Switzerland is a wonderful holiday destination for children and youngsters, and the Swiss have refined the art of looking after their needs and preferences. Apart from the many and varied facilities for winter sports for which expert tuition is readily available, children can also choose from a vast range of year-round sports opportunities, from excellent swimming pools and skating rinks to tennis courts and miniature golf courses. They will also delight in the numerous festivals, carnivals, processions and folklore events held in towns and villages throughout the country – some of them accompanied by spectacular firework displays – while even small toddlers are well catered for at supervised kindergartens in all the major holiday resorts.

TIGHT BUDGET

One way of keeping costs down while visiting Switzerland is to avoid staying in the most

Learning to ski can be an exciting experience for active youngsters

popular and fashionable resorts, choosing, instead, the small hotels and guest houses in neighbouring villages where prices are considerably cheaper. 'Einfach & Gemütlich' (Simple and Cosy) is a voluntary chain of family-run small hotels, pensions, dormitories and mountain lodges, all in the most reasonable price category. There are 175 hotels in 143 locations, many off the beaten track, listed in the *E&G Hotel Guide* which is available (charge) from the SNTO. Cheap accommodation can often be found in private houses. Look out for the sign 'Zimmer' (in German-speaking Switzerland where most of such rooms are) or 'Chambres á louer' in French-speaking regions. In summer, efficiently-run camping sites are found near every major tourist centre.

Swiss public transport is excellent, so you should not experience much difficulty finding your way to the more up-market resorts. It is worth buying one of the various cost-saving transport cards and passes widely available (► 107).

SPECIAL EVENTS

January
Folk celebrations in most towns and villages to usher in the New Year; horse-racing on snow in St Moritz and Arosa; the *Vogel Gryff* festival in Basel; International Lauberhorn ski races in Wengen.

February
Famous Basel carnival, beginning on the Monday after Ash Wednesday; *Fritschi* festival in Luzern, beginning the Thursday before Ash Wednesday; procession of

harlequins in Schwyz; *Mardi Gras* in the Ticino; speed skating championships in Davos.

March

Engadine cross-country ski marathon; Parsenn Derby downhill ski race at Davos; footwashing ceremonies on Maundy Thursday in numerous Catholic communities; religious processions in many southern towns on Good Friday.

April

Festa delle Camelie at Locarno; *Sechseläuten* festival of Zürich, featuring a parade and bonfire; blessing of horses, donkeys and mules at Tourtemagne on 23 April; start of the *Primavera Concertistica* classical music festival in Lugano.

May

Festival of the *Feuillu* on the first Sunday in May at Catigny, Geneva; procession headed by the Grenadiers of God at Kippel, in the Valais; Spring Musical Festival in Neuchâtel; beginning of festival of music and ballet in Lausanne; Golden Rose Television Festival at Montreux.

June

Rose Week in Geneva; International June Festival in Zürich; Art Festival in Bern; High Alpine ballooning at Mürren.

July

Rose Festival of Weggis; crossbow shooting in the Emmental; giant slalom on the Diablerets' glacier and summer ski race on the Jungfraujoch; International Jazz Festival of Montreux; Nyon Folk Music Festival.

August

Swiss National Day celebrations throughout the country on 1 August, with firework displays a feature; Geneva Festival, featuring fireworks and parades; music festival in Luzern and film festival in Locarno; folk festivals at Interlaken; Yehudi Menuhin festival at Gstaad.

September

Shooting contest in Zürich; torchlight religious processions at Einsiedeln; music festival in Montreux (also at the end of August and beginning of October).

October

Garden show in Geneva; agricultural and dairy show at St Gallen; Italian Opera Festival in Lausanne; vintage festivals in wine-growing regions.

November

Numerous open-air markets throughout Switzerland, that at Bern, the Zibelemârit (onion market), with public festivities, being one of the most fascinating.

December

World-famous ice hockey tournament in Davos; *Escalade*, an ancient custom, in Geneva on 11 and 12 December, with torchlight processions; numerous festivals on St Nicholas Day, 6 December.

SPORT

Winter sports are, of course, the main activities sought by visitors to Switzerland. For information on facilities available see the entries for individual resorts. However, there are also plenty of other ways of using up energy.

Cycling Bicycles can be hired from Swiss Federal Railway stations and some of the private railway administrations.

Advance reservations should be made directly to the station booking office.

Fishing In Switzerland's countless streams, rivers and lakes the angler will find plenty of exciting sport. Restocking of lake, brook, brown and rainbow trout as well as grayling and pike is done every year. As the fishing regulations vary from one place to another, it is best to enquire about licences and regulations at the hotel or local tourist offices.

Hiking Local walking and excursion maps are obtainable at the tourist offices of most resorts, and Ordnance Survey maps can be ordered through the Swiss National Tourist Office. Suggestions for eight walking tours across Switzerland are included in a leaflet *Walking Tours in Switzerland* and obtainable from the SNTO.

Mountaineering The most

Few places offer a more spectacular backdrop for paragliding than the Swiss Alps

challenging peaks of the entire Alpine region are in Switzerland. In summer, as in winter, they offer many attractive goals to which access has been facilitated by some 150 mountain huts which various branches of the Swiss Alpine Club have built.

You can learn the intricacies of the technique of mountain climbing at the mountaineering schools in Andermatt, Champéry, Les Collons, Davos, Les Diablerets, Disentis, Engelberg, Fiesch, La Fouly, Glarus, Grindelwald, Kandersteg, Klosters, Meiringen, Pontresina, Raron, Riederalp, Saas-Fee, Saas-Grund, Sils (Engadine), Thun, Urnâsch, Verbier and Zermatt. Guides are also available at many other resorts.

It is important to remember, however, that excellent physical condition and appropriate equipment are essential, and that on no account should a climb be attempted without a guide.

Tennis/Squash There is hardly a Swiss resort without tennis courts (some indoors) and squash courts. Many hotels maintain their own courts.

Watersports Opportunities for swimming are found at all altitudes. Lidos have been established by lakes and rivers, and numerous indoor and outdoor artificial pools have been built for the enjoyment of holidaymakers. Most bathing lidos are open from June until September, even longer in warmer regions. Many hotels also have heated swimming pools open throughout the year.

Swimming has a special appeal against the backdrop of Swiss mountains

Practical Matters

Above: *Zürich tram*
Right: *the scenic route of the train to Zermatt*

GLACIER
EXPRESS
St.Moritz–Reichenau–Andermatt–Brig
Zermatt
Züge 534/903   Standort: Brig FO

TIME DIFFERENCES

| GMT 12 noon | Switzerland → 1PM | Germany → 1PM | USA (NY) ← 7AM | Netherlands → 1PM | Spain → 1PM |

BEFORE YOU GO

WHAT YOU NEED

- ● Required
- ○ Suggested
- ▲ Not required

	UK	Germany	USA	Netherlands	Spain
Passport	●	●	●	●	●
Visa	▲	▲	▲	▲	▲
Onward or Return Ticket	▲	▲	▲	▲	▲
Health Inoculations	▲	▲	▲	▲	▲
Health Documentation (➤ 123, Health)	▲	▲	▲	▲	▲
Travel Insurance	○	○	○	○	○
Driving Licence (national)	●	●	●	●	●
Car Insurance Certificate (if own car)	●	●	●	●	●
Car Registration Document (if own car)	●	●	●	●	●

WHEN TO GO

Zürich

  High season

Low season

2°C	4°C	8°C	12°C	18°C	21°C	22°C	22°C	18°C	13°C	6°C	2°C
JAN	FEB	MAR	APR	MAY	JUN	JUL	AUG	SEP	OCT	NOV	DEC

 Cloud   Sun   Sunshine/Showers

TOURIST OFFICES

In the UK
Swiss Centre
Swiss Court
London W1V 8EE
☎ 020 7437 4577

In the USA
Swiss Centre
608 Fifth Avenue
New York
NY 10020
☎ (212) 757 5944
Fax: (212) 262 6116

Swiss Centre
222 Sepulveda Boulevard
El Segundo
Los Angeles
CA 90245
☎ (310) 335 5985
Fax: (310) 335 5982

POLICE 117

FIRE 118

AMBULANCE 144

AVALANCHE BULLETIN 187

WHEN YOU ARE THERE

ARRIVING

Switzerland has three international airports, at Basel, Geneva and Zürich. There are also many domestic airports and a good internal flight system.

Zürich Airport Distance to city centre	Journey times
12km	🚆 10 minutes
	🚌 20 minutes
	🚐 15 minutes

Geneva Airport Distance to city centre	Journey times
5km	🚆 6 minutes
	🚌 20 minutes
	🚐 15 minutes

MONEY

Switzerland's currency is the Swiss franc, issued in 1,000, 200, 100, 50, 20 and 10 franc notes, and 5, 2, 1 and ½ franc coins. There are 100 centimes in a franc, and 20, 10 and 5 centime coins. Traveller's cheques are accepted by most hotels, shops and restaurants in lieu of cash, but the rate of exchange may be less favourable than in banks. Traveller's cheques issued in Swiss francs are most convenient.
Banks can be found in all towns and most villages and handle traveller's cheques, Eurocheques and give cash advances on credit cards.

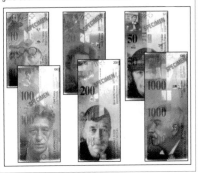

TIME

 Switzerland is one hour ahead of Greenwich mean time (GMT + 1), but from March to October daylight saving time (GMT + 2) operates, as in the UK.

CUSTOMS

➡ **YES**

Visitors from European Countries
Alcohol: up to 15% vol – 2 litres; over 15% vol – 1 litre
Tobacco: 200 cigarettes AND 50 cigars AND 250g pipe tobacco
Perfume: No limit

Visitors from Non-European Countries
Alcohol: up to 15% – vol 2 litres; over 15% vol – 1 litre
Tobacco: 400 cigarettes AND 100 cigars AND 250g pipe tobacco
Perfume: No limit

Visitors must be aged at least 17 to benefit from tobacco and alcohol allowances.

⊖ **NO**

Drugs, firearms, offensive weapons, obscene material.

EMBASSIES

UK
(031) 352 5021

Germany
(031) 359 4111

USA
(031) 357 7011

Netherlands
(031) 352 7063

Spain
(031) 352 04

WHEN YOU ARE THERE

TOURIST OFFICES

Basel
- Schifflände 5
  CH-4001 Basel
  ☎ (061) 268 6868
  Fax: (061) 268 6870
  www.baseltourismus.ch

Bern
- Im Bahnhof
  CH-3011 Bern
  ☎ (031) 328 1212
  Fax: (031) 312 1233
  www.berntourismus.ch

Geneva
- rue du Mont-Blanc 3
  CH-1201 Genève
  ☎ (022) 909 7000
  Fax: (022) 909 7011
  www.geneva-tourism.ch

Zürich
- Im Hauptbahnhof
  CH-8023 Zürich
  ☎ (01) 215 4000
  Fax: (01) 215 4044
  www. zurichtourism.ch

Other useful websites:
Switzerland Tourism
www.switzerlandvacation.ch

Information about Switzerland
www.about.ch

The Swiss Embassy in the US
www.swissemb.org

Bernese Oberland
www.berneroberland.com

Valais
www.matterhornstate.com

For skiers
www.skiin.com

NATIONAL HOLIDAYS

J	F	M	A	M	J	J	A	S	O	N	D
2	2			1		1		2	1	2	1

1 Jan	New Year's Day
Mar/Apr	Good Friday
	Easter Monday
May	Ascension Day
	Whit Monday
1 Aug	National Day
25 Dec	Christmas Day
26 Dec	Boxing Day

There are also individual canton holidays, usually 2 Jan, 1 May, Corpus Christi (late May/early June) and Thanksgiving (Sep).

OPENING HOURS

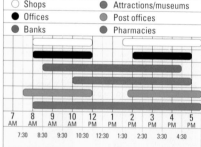

○ Shops ● Attractions/museums
● Offices ○ Post offices
● Banks ● Pharmacies

7AM 8AM 9AM 10AM 12PM 1PM 2PM 3PM 4PM 5PM
7:30 8:30 9:30 10:30 12:30 1:30 2:30 3:30 4:30

The times given above apply Monday to Friday. On Saturdays shops and pharmacies close at 4 and post offices at 11AM. Large department stores, super-markets and shops in tourist areas may open outside the times shown, especially in summer (and winter in winter-sport areas).
Museums are usually open until 9PM on one day each week, and closed on one day a week, usually Monday.

DRIVE ON THE RIGHT

TOILETS FREE

PUBLIC TRANSPORT

 Internal Flights Switzerland has a superb domestic air service operated by Swissair and its domestic arm, Crossair. You will need to book ahead at the height of the summer and winter seasons. For airport information ring: Basel (061) 325 2511; Bern (031) 960 2111; Geneva (022) 717 7111; Zürich (01) 157 1060

 Trains Switzerland has one of the best railway systems in Europe. The system offers a number of savings to visitors. The Swiss Pass gives a 25 per cent reduction on services (rail, bus or boat) with validity from four days to one month. The Swiss Flexi Pass allows the visitor to choose three discounted travel days from a 15-day period. The Swiss Card gives a 50 per cent reduction on travel from your airport to your destination and back and reductions on rail, bus and boats. It is valid for one month. There are also regional passes and Family Cards.

 Buses Switzerland has an excellent bus service. Of particular interest to walkers is the Postbus service, which visits even remote alpine villages. These operate to a reliable timetable. Postbuses are yellow and marked by a post horn on a black disc. Their horns play the first notes of Rossini's *William Tell Overture*.

 Ferries The larger lakes have steamer services. There is a Boat Pass available that entitles visitors to a 50 per cent discount for one or two weeks.

CAR RENTAL

 All the major car-hire companies are represented at Swiss airports and railway stations, and have offices in the major towns and cities. Hire cars usually already have a motorway tax (*vignette*).

TAXIS

 Taxis are available at all airports, railway and bus stations, and at key places in large towns and cities.

DRIVING

 Speed limit on motorways: **120kph** If you are planning to drive on Swiss motorways in your own car you must display a *vignette* (tax sticker) – or risk a fine. It costs Sfr40 and is available at border crossings, post offices and service stations, or in advance from your Swiss Tourist Office.

 Speed limit on main roads: **80kph** Speed limit on minor roads: **50kph**

 Speed limit in urban areas: **50kph**

 Seat belts are obligatory for drivers and all passengers over the age of seven. Children under 12 years must travel in rear seats.

 Random breath testing is carried out. Limit: 80μg of alcohol in 100ml of breath.

 Petrol stations keep shop hours (though they may be open later in the evening). Even motorway petrol stations close at night. Most petrol stations take credit cards.

 A red warning triangle must be carried and its use is obligatory in case of breakdown or accident. If you break down, the Touring Club of Switzerland (TCS) (022) 417 2727 and the Swiss Automobile Club (ACS) (031) 311 7722, offer a breakdown service. If your car is hired, follow the instructions.

Ruler markings:
CENTIMETRES 0 1 2 3 4 5 6 7 8
INCHES 0 1 2 3

PERSONAL SAFETY

Switzerland is generally a safe place for tourists, with the greatest risk coming from tourists, but to help prevent crime:

- Do not carry around more cash than you need.
- Do not leave valuables at the poolside.
- Beware of pickpockets in tourist spots or crowded places.
- Avoid walking alone at night in dark alleys in large cities.

Switzerland has several police forces, with a federal force as well as cantonal ones. If you need a police station ask for *die Polizei* (in German-speaking parts), *la Police* (French) or *la Polizia* (Italian).

Police assistance:
☎ **117**
from any call box

TELEPHONES

Public telephones take both coins and cards (PTT phonecards). Coins from 5 centimes to 2 francs can be used, but the minimum amount for a local call is 60 centimes, Sfr 1 for a national call, and Sfr 5 for an international call. Phonecards of various values can be obtained from post offices and many shops. Calls are usually more expensive from hotels.

The cheap rate for calls 18.00–08.00 hrs Monday to Friday, and all day Saturday and Sunday.

The country code for Switzerland is 41.

International Dialling Codes	
from Switzerland to:	
UK:	00 44
Germany:	00 49
USA:	00 1
Netherlands:	00 31

POST

Post offices (*Postamt* in German, *la Poste* in French, *la Posta* in Italian) are open Monday to Friday 7:30–12 and 1:45–6:30; Saturday 7:30–11. Major offices may be open later on Saturdays.

Correspondence can be forwarded to Swiss post offices for collection – clearly mark the envelope 'Poste restante', and make sure you put the postcode before the name of the town. To collect a letter the addressee should produce his/her passport as proof of identity.

ELECTRICITY

The power supply in Switzerland is 220 volts. Sockets accept two-round-pin plugs, so an adaptor is needed for most non-Continental appliances and a transformer for appliances operating on 100–120 volts.

TIPS/GRATUITIES

Yes ✓ No ✗		
Restaurants (usually included)	✓	10%
Cafés/bars	✓	Change
Tour guides	✓	2 francs
Taxis (usually included)	✓	10%
Porters	✓	1 franc
Chambermaids	✓	1 franc
Usherettes	✓	Change
Hairdressers	✓	Change
Cloakroom attendants	✓	Change
Toilets	✗	

PHOTOGRAPHY
What to photograph: buildings in the old town centres, alpine villages, mountains, the magnificent views
Best time to photograph: all day. The mountains look especially good in early morning light and at sunset.
Where to buy film: films and camera batteries are readily available in tourist and photographic shops.

HEALTH

Insurance
Switzerland does not have a state health system so visitors are strongly advised to take out medical insurance.

Dental Services
There is no state dental service so visitors are strongly advised to take out medical insurance that covers dental care.

Sun Advice
In southern Switzerland especially the summers are hot so visitors should take precautions against the sun. In winter the sun is stronger than it seems because of the altitude of most winter sports resorts, so again take precautions against burning.

Drugs
Medicines for personal use only are allowed through customs. Many prescription and non-prescription drugs are available from pharmacies.

Safe Water
Swiss tap water is completely safe to drink. However, because of the sterilisation processes many people buy mineral water, which is readily available everywhere.

CONCESSIONS

There are no special student or senior citizen concessions on offer in Switzerland. Discounted travel cards are available to all.

CLOTHING SIZES

USA	UK	Europe	
36	36	46	
38	38	48	
40	40	50	
42	42	52	Suits
44	44	54	
46	46	56	
8	7	41	
8.5	7.5	42	
9.5	8.5	43	
10.5	9.5	44	Shoes
11.5	10.5	45	
12	11	46	
14.5	14.5	37	
15	15	38	
15.5	15.5	39/40	
16	16	41	Shirts
16.5	16.5	42	
17	17	43	
6	8	34	
8	10	36	
10	12	38	
12	14	40	Dresses
14	16	42	
16	18	44	
6	4.5	38	
6.5	5	38	
7	5.5	39	
7.5	6	39	Shoes
8	6.5	40	
8.5	7	41	

WHEN DEPARTING

- Remember to contact the airport on the day prior to leaving to ensure the flight details are unchanged
- Swiss customs officials are usually polite, but will stick to the strict letter of the law

LANGUAGE

Most of the country, particularly the north, east and central areas, is German-speaking. However, Swiss German (Schwyzerdütsch) is a form of old German and has numerous differences from modern German. It also has several local dialects. French is spoken in the west of the country (though in many parts of the west the people also speak German). Italian is confined to the canton of Ticino and the southern tips of the Grisons. Romansch, Switzerland's fourth official language, is spoken in parts of the Grisons. Below are some useful words and phrases in the three main languages.

		German	French	Italian
ACCOMMODATION	hotel	Hotel, Pension	hôtel	albergo
	single room	Einzelzimmer	pour une personne	singola
	double room	Doppelzimmer	pour deux personnes	matrimoniale
	one night	eine Nacht	une nuit	una notte
	reservation	Reservierung	réservation	prenotazione
	bath	Bad	salle de bain	bagno
	shower	Dusche	douche	doccia
MONEY	bank	Bank	banque	banca
	exchange office	Geldwechsel	bureau de change	cambio
	bank note	Schein	billet	banconote
	traveller's cheque	Reisescheck	chèque-voyage	traveller's cheque
	credit card	Kreditkarte	carte de crédit	carta di credito
	post office	Postamt	poste	posta
EATING OUT	breakfast	Frühstück	petit déjeuner	colazione
	lunch	Mittagessen	déjeuner	pranzo
	dinner	Abendessen	dîner	cena
	table	Tisch	table	tavolo
	starter	Vorspeise	entrée	antipasto
	main course	Hauptspeise	plat de résistance	piatto
	bill	Rechnung	l'addition	conto
TRAVEL	airport	Flughafen	aéroport	aeroporto
	train	Zug	train	treno
	station	Bahnhof	gare	stazione
	boat	Boot	bateau	battello
	single ticket	einfache Fahrkarte	aller	andante
	return ticket	Rückfahrkarte	aller-retour	andante e ritorno
	non-smoking	Nichtraucher	non fumer	non fuma
USEFUL PHRASES	yes	ja	oui	si
	no	nein	non	non
	please	bitte	s'il vous plaît	per favore
	thank you	danke	merci	grazie
	good morning	guten Morgen	bonjour	buongiorno
	you're welcome	bitte	de rien	prego
	do you speak English?	sprechen sie Englisch?	parlez-vous anglais?	parla inglese?
	open	offen	ouvert	aperto

INDEX

Acknowledgements

The Automobile Association would like to thank the following libraries for their assistance in the compilation of this book.

MARY EVANS PICTURE LIBRARY 8b

J ALLAN CASH PHOTOLIBRARY 19, 49, 70, 87, 102.

MRI BANKERS' GUIDE TO FOREIGN CURRENCY 105.

INTERNATIONAL PHOTOBANK 20, 23, 26, 31, 33, 40, 45, 47, 60, 68, 77, 79, 80, 86, 94

NATURE PHOTOGRAPHERS LTD 90 (P R Sterry), 93 (P R Sterry).

SPECTRUM COLOUR LIBRARY Front cover (national costume of Luzern), 13, 15, 36, 55, 66, 84,97

THE STOCK MARKET 25, 35, 56, 64, 65, 82, 99.

TANIA TANG/WTO 9

CAROL WEITZ 108a, 108b

The remaining photographs are held in the Association's own library (AA PHOTO LIBRARY), with contributions from:

ADRIAN BAKER Back cover, 2, 7b, 51, 53, 58, 62, 101, 103b; STEVE DAY Front cover (mountain village, astronomical clock), 1, 4a, 4b, 5a, 5b, 6a, 6b, 7a, 7c, 8a, 9a, 10, 11, 39, 42/43, 72, 73, 96, 103a

Contributors
This edition revised by Richard Sale. Additional text by Richard Sale.